The Science of Sound

Pitch, Volume, Music, and Noise

with Hands-On Science Activities for Kids

ANDI DIEHN

Illustrated by Micah Rauch

More science titles from Nomad Press

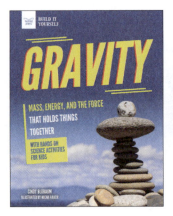 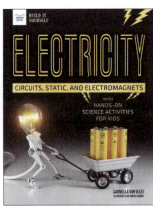 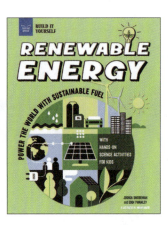 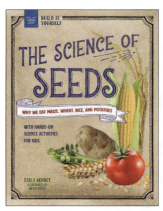

Check out more titles at www.nomadpress.net

Nomad Press
A division of Nomad Communications
10 9 8 7 6 5 4 3 2 1
Copyright © 2025 by Nomad Press. All rights reserved.

No part of this book may be reproduced in any form without permission in writing from the publisher, except by a reviewer who may quote brief passages in a review or **for limited educational use**. The trademark "Nomad Press" and the Nomad Press logo are trademarks of Nomad Communications, Inc.

This book was manufactured by Versa Press, East Peoria, Illinois
June 2025, Job #J25-00981
ISBN Softcover: 978-1-61930-996-8
ISBN Hardcover: 978-1-61930-993-7

Educational Consultant, Marla Conn

Questions regarding the ordering of this book should be addressed to
Nomad Press
PO Box 1036, Norwich, VT 05055
www.nomadpress.net

Printed in the United States.

CONTENTS

Timeline... iv

Introduction
What's in a Sound?... 1

Chapter 1
Super Sound Waves... 13

Chapter 2
Heroic Hearing... 33

Chapter 3
Pitch Perfect... 48

Chapter 4
All That Sound... 62

Chapter 5
Sound Technology... 78

Glossary

Metric Conversions

Selected Bibliography

Essential Questions

Resources

Index

Interested in primary sources? Look for this icon.

Some of the QR codes in this book link to primary sources that offer firsthand information about the topic. Photos are often considered primary sources because a photograph takes a picture at the moment something happens—but watch out for fake ones! Use a smartphone or tablet app to scan the QR code and explore more. You can find a list of the URLs on the Resources page. You can also use the suggested keywords to find other helpful sources.

🔎 sound

TIMELINE

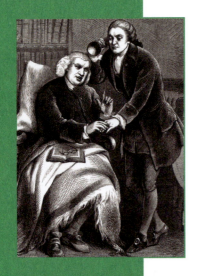

C.* 550 BCE: An ancient Greek named Pythagoras describes the connection between the pitch of a vibrating string and its length.

C. 350 BCE: Ancient Greek thinker Aristotle suggests that sound travels through the air to our ears.

C. 500 CE: Ancient Roman thinker Boethius compares sound waves to ripples of water.

1500: Italian artist and inventor Leonardo da Vinci suggests sound travels in waves.

1635: French philosopher Pierre Gassendi conducts the first experiments on the speed of sound.

1638: Italian thinker Galileo Galilei conducts tests that show the connection between pitch and frequency.

1660: Irish and English physicists Robert Boyle and Robert Hooke show sound must travel through a medium such as air.

1668: English scientist Isaac Newton conducts experiments demonstrating the speed of sound.

1793: Italian scientist Lazzaro Spallanzani is the first person to suggest bats hear sounds that people cannot.

1842: Austrian physicist Christian Doppler describes changes in wave frequency that depend on how a source of waves and an observer move toward or away from each other.

1883: British scientist Francis Galton observes that cats and dogs hear sounds we can't and invents the ultrasonic whistle.

1876: American inventor Alexander Graham Bell patents the telephone after figuring out how to convert sound waves from human speech into an electrical current and back.

1880: Alexander Graham Bell establishes the Volta Laboratory Association, an electro-acoustic research facility.

*When scholars do not know the exact year of an event, they use the word circa, or its short form c in front of the date. Circa means "about."

TIMELINE

1885: Welsh singer and scientist Megan Watts Hughes invents the eidophone, a device that transforms sound into visual patterns.

1887: Austrian physicist Ernst Mach figures out how to calculate the speed of sound, which is named Mach in his honor.

1895: American anthropologist Alice Cunningham Fletcher records the music of Native American tribes on wax cylinders.

1906: American naval architect Lewis Nixon invents sonar to detect icebergs, and the technology is later used during WWI (1914–1918) to detect submarines.

1925: Scientists, using sonar, detect the Mid-Atlantic Ridge, a massive mountain range in the Atlantic Ocean.

1925: Electric microphones, speakers, and recorders produce and record sound.

1930s: Canadian-American Helen Oakley Dance becomes the first female record producer.

1945: Scientists make sound recordings on magnetic tapes for the first time.

1947: American pilot Chuck Yeager is the first person to break the sound barrier, flying the rocket-powered Bell X-1, an experimental aircraft.

1958: English physician Ian Donald uses ultrasound imaging to look inside the body.

1990: The U.S. Food and Drug Administration approves cochlear implants for children ages 2 to 17.

2016: More than 450,000 people have received cochlear implants worldwide.

2020s: Immersive audio technology means people can listen to performances with headphones and feel as if they're in the concert space.

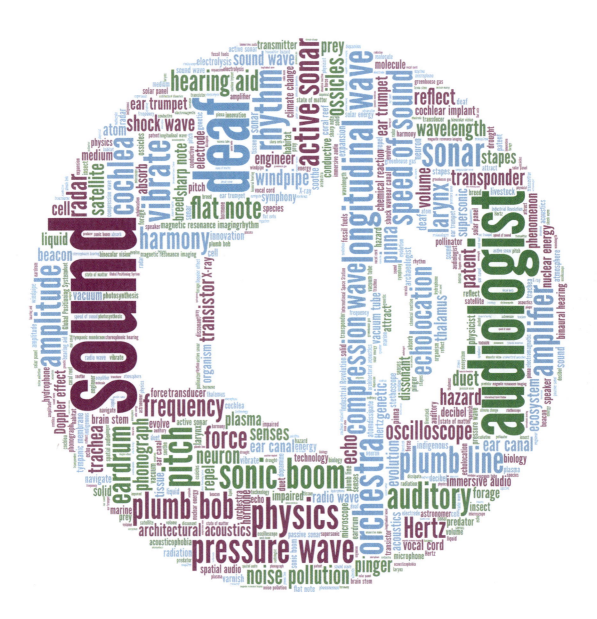

Introduction

WHAT'S IN A
SOUND?

Imagine exploring a wooded park. Squirrels chatter and race over crunchy leaves. Songbirds tweet from leafy branches. Children rush by, clomping their feet, to see the dancing jets of water in the fountain. Burble, burble, whoosh!

A fountain is a fun place to—SPLASH! Children jump, skip, and stomp while clapping their hands to the beat of their feet and joining in the **symphony** of **sounds**. Maybe someone brought a harmonica to the park—what kinds of sounds does it make? Do you hear the hum of conversations happening among the people around you? Listen to the rolling skateboards, zipping bikes, and pounding sneakers. How many sounds can you hear?

ESSENTIAL QUESTION

Why is sound an important part of most people's lives?

THE SCIENCE OF SOUND

WORDS TO KNOW

symphony: a piece of music written for an orchestra.

sound: vibrations that travel through matter, which is any substance that has mass and takes up space, such as air, water, and wood.

orchestra: a group of musicians that play a variety of instruments.

soothe: to make someone feel calm.

energy: the power to work and move.

solar energy: energy from the sun.

livestock: animals raised for food and other uses.

photosynthesis: the process plants use to convert the sun's energy into food.

chemical reaction: a process where one or more substances are chemically changed and transformed into different substances.

nuclear reaction: when atoms fuse together or split apart. This releases a large amount of energy.

SOUND IS ALL AROUND YOU

For many people, the world is an **orchestra** of sound, from sunup to sundown. When we wake, we hear the buzz of an alarm, footsteps, voices, and the clank of breakfast dishes. During the day, cars honk, desks and chairs squeak, and friends chat and laugh. At night, the fridge hums, water in pipes gurgles, and owls may hoot.

There are many other kinds of sounds, too. Sounds in nature tend to be pleasing. The wind moves leafy tree branches. It makes them rustle. Raindrops pitter and patter onto umbrellas. These sounds **soothe**. They are beautiful to hear. Animals make an array of sounds, from squeaks and squawks to honks and tiny buzzes. All kinds of creatures use sound to communicate.

How many sounds do you think are happening in this amusement park?

WHAT'S IN A SOUND?

Musicians create sounds with instruments for us to enjoy. They pluck the strings of guitars. Pling! They blow into flutes with a tootle-to. Machines produce sounds. They ding, rattle, and bang. People make sounds, too. The average person hears between 20,000 and 30,000 words per day!

Listen to the sounds of the National Parks on this website. How many different sounds can you hear? Do these places sound different from the area around your home?

National Park sounds

Now that we have looked at a few sounds, let's find out exactly what sound is.

ENERGY!

Sound is a type of **energy**. Energy makes things move and change all around us. The human body needs energy to grow, keep warm, and laugh. Whether we kick a ball, leap into a pool, or play running games at recess, our bodies break down food to release energy for us to play.

Try this! Hold a plastic ruler on the edge of a table. Pluck it with your other hand. When do you hear the sound? Predict what will happen if more of the ruler rests on the table. Pluck the ruler. Was your prediction correct? What happened?

Energy from the sun warms our planet. This is called **solar energy**. It helps us grow healthy food such as the fruit and vegetables that feed both humans and **livestock**. **Photosynthesis** is the process plants use to convert sunlight into the energy they need to grow.

Humans use solar energy in other ways. People collect solar energy with roof panels to create electricity. Millions of homes light up because of this electricity. Energy also comes from the wind and from **chemical** and **nuclear reactions**.

THE SCIENCE OF SOUND

WORDS TO KNOW

vibrate: when an object shakes up and down or back and forth.

phenomenon: something seen or observed. Plural is phenomena.

conductive: describes a material that carries electricity easily.

attract: when an invisible **force** pulls things together.

force: a push or pull that changes an object's motion.

matter: any substance that has mass and takes up space, such as air, water, and wood.

atom: the tiniest building block of matter.

molecule: the smallest amount of something.

technology: tools, methods, and systems used to solve a problem or do work.

microscope: a tool that helps scientists look at objects invisible to the bare eye.

All sounds, from the chirp of insects to the meow of a cat, begin with energy. A door doesn't make a sound on its own. Your hand needs to move it. When you pull the door open, it **vibrates** and your ears hear a creak. When you push it shut, the door vibrates again and your ears hear a firm click. Sometimes, the sound from a door might begin with energy from the wind. The door closes with a bang when the wind whisks it shut. The energy from the door creates a back-and-forth or up-and-down movement called a vibration, which travels through the air to our ears, where we hear it as sound.

Let's find out how the sound vibrations travel to your ears.

Underwater Sounds

Long ago, people didn't know if sound traveled in liquid. So, French scientist and priest Jean-Antoine Nollet (1700-1790) conducted sound experiments in a river. He discovered he could hear sounds, including a bell, underwater.

Nollet was also interested in electricity and did many early experiments to learn more about this **phenomenon**. He even suspended people from the ceiling using **conductive** silk rope and electrified them, causing the person to build up a charge and **attract** things. It's the same thing that happens when you rub a balloon on your head for a while and then stick it to a wall. But don't worry, people who helped with Nollet's experiment weren't hurt!

WHAT'S IN A SOUND?

The bow makes the strings on this cello vibrate, and that vibration produces sound.

MATTER AND MOLECULES

Sound travels from a source such as a bell, a band, or a waterfall to the ear through **matter**. Matter is everywhere. Just about everything we see is made of matter. Your chair, the table, this book, your worn-in shoes and a favorite soft blanket—all of this is matter. It's everything we touch. You are made of matter, too!

Matter is made up of teeny building blocks called **atoms**. When atoms join with one or more atoms, they form larger particles called **molecules**. A molecule of water, for example, is made of two hydrogen atoms and one oxygen atom. Molecules are much too small for humans to see without advanced **technology**. They can't be seen even with a regular **microscope**.

What isn't made of matter? Your thoughts and emotions—can you weigh or touch them? No! Can you weigh or measure light? No! These things aren't made of matter. Can you think of others?

Learn more about how sound travels underwater in this video. Why do you have more trouble understanding your friend's words underwater than on land?

🔍 Discovery sound travels

5

THE SCIENCE OF SOUND

WORDS TO KNOW

sound wave: an invisible vibration in the air that you hear as sound.

state of matter: the form that matter takes. The four states of matter are solid, liquid, gas, and plasma.

solid: a state of matter with a definite shape.

liquid: a state of matter that takes the form of its container and has a fixed **volume**.

volume: the amount of space an object takes up.

gas: a state of matter in which atoms and molecules are spread far apart.

plasma: a state of matter similar to a gas but with temperatures and pressures so high that electrons are stripped away from their atoms and move freely. It is the most common form of matter in the universe.

wave: a curving movement in water, air, ground, or other object.

climate change: a change in long-term weather patterns, which can happen through natural or manmade processes.

stethoscope: a tool used by doctors to listen to sounds inside the body.

How tiny are they? A single molecule is 10 trillion times smaller than a single grain of rice!

How do the molecules in sound begin moving? Something must vibrate to get them moving. Imagine yourself plucking the strings of a guitar. Twang! The strings vibrate each time you pluck them. The strings' vibrations kick off a reaction similar to bumper cars—the molecules bump into the ones next to them, causing them to vibrate.

The vibrating molecules create a **sound wave** that carries the sound from the object to the ear. We'll learn more about sound waves in Chapter 1.

THREE STATES

There are four **states of matter**—**solid**, **liquid**, **gas**, and **plasma**. An ice cube is a solid substance until it melts and becomes a liquid. As time passes, some of the liquid water will turn to gas in a process called evaporation. Much of the sun is made of plasma. Lightning strikes create plasma, too!

Sound travels more easily when the molecules in the matter it's traveling through are closer together. That means sound travels quickly through a solid, less quickly through a liquid, and slowest through a gas.

To model a solid, imagine a group of people standing in a marching band, locking arms so they are all stuck together. There's not a lot of room to move and vibrate, so sound waves will slip through without using a lot of energy.

WHAT'S IN A SOUND?

A model of a liquid is like a very crowded room. People are moving around, but they are still practically touching each other. There's more room between them than there was when they were a solid, but sound waves still travel pretty easily through the crowd.

> **Learn more about sound with this video.** How can you show that sound travels in **waves**?
>
> curious crew sound vibrations

In a gas, people have a lot more room to move. A person can spin their way across the room without bumping into too many other people. That means sound waves have to work harder to make the leap from molecule to molecule. Those waves are going to move a lot more slowly.

> **What would it be like to listen through a wall? Rest an ear on a wall and tap on it. What do you notice?**

In this book, you'll explore the loudest sounds in history. We'll also talk about the quietest areas on Earth. One place is so quiet, people can hear their eyeballs squelching in their heads!

You'll also discover how scientists use sound to explore the ocean, look inside the body, and study **climate change**. Plus, make some career connections in the field of sound. Along the way, you'll turn glasses into a musical instrument, a bowl into your eardrum, and a tube into a **stethoscope**. Ready? Let's go catch some sound waves!

Essential Questions

Each chapter of this book begins with an essential question to help guide your exploration of sound. Keep the question in your mind as you read the chapter. At the end of each chapter, use your science notebook (you'll make that next!) to record your thoughts and answers.

> **ESSENTIAL QUESTION**
>
> Why is sound an important part of most people's lives?

MAKE A
SCIENCE NOTEBOOK

For scientists and engineers, notebooks are very important tools. That's where they write down their observations and record their data. It's also where they keep track of their experiments, often by using the scientific method (which you'll learn about on page 10). Make your own science notebook to use as you do the experiments in this book!

> **Cover the notebook front and back with the patterned paper and cardstock and secure with glue.** Set to one side.

> **From the plain paper, cut out a label roughly one-third the size of the notebook.** Write your name on the label and add any details and drawings you'd like with your colored pencils and washi tape.

> **Cut the ribbon long enough to wrap around your notebook.** Glue the ribbon down across the front and back of the notebook so it can be tied closed at the opening edge.

TOOL KIT
- a composition notebook
- assorted patterned paper and cardstock
- scissors
- glue
- 1 sheet of plain paper
- colored pencils
- washi tape (optional)
- ribbon
- pencil

Italian artist and inventor Leonardo da Vinci (1452–1519) was known as a visionary. He did many experiments and built many models trying to understand the world. And he kept many notebooks! Take a look at Leonardo's notebook on this website. How is it different seeing his writing and drawings as opposed to reading them typed out? Do you learn something different?

🔍 Leonardo da Vinci notebook

Try This!

Leonardo da Vinci kept his notebooks safe even as he worked and traveled throughout Europe. How can your notebook be kept safe during your sound investigations?

TEXT TO WORLD
What are some ways you protect yourself from noises that are too loud? How about sounds that never seem to stop? How do you control the sounds you hear?

COLLECT SOUNDS

TOOL KIT
- science notebook and pencil
- recording device

A laugh and a sneeze. Achoo! A song on the radio and the ding of the doorbell. Sounds surround us. It's important to be aware of the sounds around you, as they can give you clues about what's going on in your environment. How many sounds can you collect in this activity?

> **Explore your home when it is quiet.** Write down every sound you hear in your science notebook.

> **Write down two adjectives describing the sound.** Some examples include loud, ferocious, whispery, hollow, stuttering, smooth, and constant.

> **Use one of the adjectives in a sentence to describe the sound.**

> **Record the sound.** You will use these recordings in the next activity.

The Kelso Dunes in the Mojave Desert in California make a unique sound. Watch this video to learn more about these singing dunes! Do you have anything like this where you live? How can you show that sound travels in waves?

🔍 Nat Geo singing dunes

THINK MORE!
Your ears send sound signals to your brain. Then, your brain tells you what the sound is. How do you think these signals travel? Learn more about this process in Chapter 2.

Try This!

Make a list of five human noises, such as laughing, in your science notebook. How do the sounds we make help us understand each other?

9

WHAT'S THAT SOUND?

TOOL KIT
- science notebook and pencil
- recording device

You've studied the sounds around you and recorded some of them. Now, it's time to play a game with these sounds. Can you tell the sounds apart?

This activity is done with a partner.

> Ask your partner to sit quietly.

> Play one sound at a time from the recordings you made in the last activity.

> Can your partner guess the sound?

> After your partner has correctly identified three sounds, switch places and repeat the experiment.

Try This!

Could you tell which object each sound belonged to? What sounds could you identify more easily? Did you both identify the same sounds?

The Scientific Method

A scientific method worksheet is a useful tool for keeping your ideas and observations organized. The scientific method is the process scientists use to ask and answer questions. Use your science notebook to make a scientific method worksheet for each experiment you do.

Question:	What are we trying to find out? What problem are we trying to solve?
Research:	What is already known about this topic?
Hypothesis:	What do we think the answer will be?
Equipment:	What supplies are we using?
Method:	What procedure are we following?
Results:	What happened and why?

SOUND DETECTIVE

> **TOOL KIT**
> - science notebook and pencil
> - colored pencils

Each outdoor space has unique sounds. How many sounds can you collect outside? It's time to become a sound detective!

› **Take a listening walk near your home.**

› **Stand as still as possible.** When you hear a sound in the environment, listen to it carefully. Ask yourself where is it coming from and what is making it.

› **Walk on until you hear your next sound and repeat step two.**

› **After your sound walk, use colored pencils to draw pictures of what made each sound in your science notebook.** You can also write a paragraph describing each sound. How are the sounds you heard different from each other? Are any of them similar?

LOCATION:
DAY:
TIME:
DESCRIPTION/DRAWING:

NOTES:

Try This!

How do the outdoor sounds compare to indoor sounds? What are some reasons for these differences?

Listen to sounds from around the world on this website. With permission from an adult, submit a sound from where you live. What are some of the differences between places that you notice?

🔍 sound cities

11

SEEING MOLECULES

TOOL KIT
- science notebook and pencil
- bag of mini marshmallows
- package of toothpicks
- sticky notes
- colored pencils

Atoms make up everything in the world. When atoms form bonds, they create molecules. Molecules are too small for you to see with your eyes, but you can build models of them.

› **Look at the diagram of a water molecule on this page.** Use the mini marshmallows and toothpicks to recreate this model. The marshmallows represent the atoms, and the toothpicks represent the bonds between the atoms. Make as many models as your supplies allow.

› **Create the three states of water on a flat surface by dividing the models up to represent water molecules in a gas, a liquid, and a solid.** Water is different from other substances. In its solid form, the hydrogen atoms of one molecule stick to the oxygen atoms of another molecule and make a three-dimensional structure of ice. This makes ice less dense than the liquid form of water. That's why ice cubes float!

> The word "sound" comes from the old French word *son*, which means "sound" or "note."

› **Which model represents a solid, a liquid, and a gas?** Write your answer in your science notebook and explain why.

› **Using the sticky notes, label the models "water vapor," "liquid water," and "ice."**

› **Add diagrams to your science notebook.**

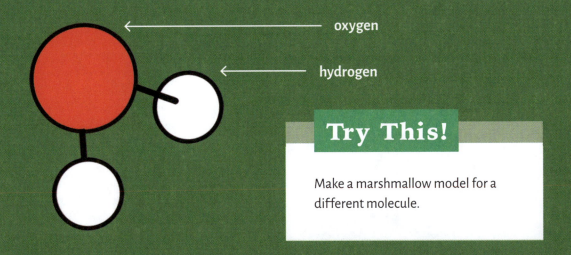

oxygen

hydrogen

Try This!

Make a marshmallow model for a different molecule.

12

Chapter 1

SUPER
SOUND WAVES

The world is full of waves. Have you seen a human wave at a ballpark? This type of wave won't get you wet, but it will get you moving. The wave begins when a group of people rise and swing their hands into the air. They cheer, *"Hooray!"* As they sit down, the group of people next to them raise their arms until the wave rolls around the stadium.

ESSENTIAL QUESTION

Why do sounds get fainter as you travel farther from the source?

How about a wave rolling through a field of wheat? You can see the direction of the wind by watching the patterns that emerge as the individual plants bend one after the other, making a scene that looks like a wave rolling along. The plants perform the same function as the people at the ballpark!

THE SCIENCE OF SOUND

WORDS TO KNOW

compression wave: waves that are pushed together by the **medium** through which they travel.

medium: a substance, such as air or water, through which energy moves.

longitudinal wave: a wave that vibrates parallel to the direction the wave is traveling.

expansion: the space between waves as they move apart.

wavelength: the distance from crest to crest in a series of waves.

frequency: the number of sound waves that pass a fixed point in a second.

pitch: how high or low a sound is, depending on its frequency.

amplitude: the strength of sound waves.

Of course, you can always see waves, big and small, at the ocean. Energy moves through the water, making the water molecules rise and fall. Although it might look as though the water is always moving forward, it's energy that's moving forward while the water stays in one general area.

ANATOMY OF A SOUND WAVE

All sound travels in waves. The sound doesn't leap directly from the object to your ears. Instead, the energy in the wave travels through matter to get to you. The matter stays in its place while the sound waves move through it. Think back to the fan wave at the ballpark. Do the fans change seats? No. The energy is what's moving in a wave, not the people.

When someone plucks a guitar string and makes a noise, the string disturbs the air molecules around it, which, in turn, disturb the air molecules around them, and so on, as the sound wave travels through the air. The molecules in a sound wave pass on energy from one molecule to the next.

A group of scientists discovered it takes at least 20 people to begin a human wave. The wave rolls around the stadium at about 20 seats per second.

Sound waves are **compression waves**, also called **longitudinal waves**. The guitar string moved forward and backward very quickly in a vibrating movement, and that forward and backward motion is reflected in the movement of the molecules around it.

SUPER SOUND WAVES

LONGITUDINAL WAVES

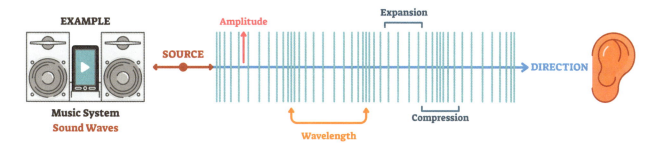

The molecules move forward and then backward very quickly, creating a pattern like the one you see above in the diagram of a sound wave. The space where the molecules are moving into each other shows compression, while the space where they're moving apart is called **expansion**. The **wavelength** is one complete cycle of compression and expansion. The **frequency** of a wave is the number of waves that pass a certain point in a given amount of time. The higher that number, the higher the frequency and the higher the **pitch**, or tone.

The **amplitude** of a wavelength measures how much energy is in the sound wave. We'll learn more about amplitude in Chapter 4.

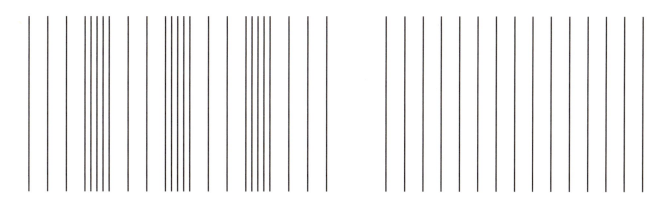

Wave A
(higher frequency, higher pitch)

Wave B
(lower frequency, lower pitch)

15

THE SCIENCE OF SOUND

WORDS TO KNOW

physicist: a scientist who studies physical forces, including matter, energy, and motion, and how these forces interact with each other.

engineer: someone who uses science, math, and creativity to design and build things.

astronomer: a person who studies objects in the sky such as the sun, moon, planets, and stars.

acoustics: a branch of science that studies sound and sound waves.

vacuum: a space without air or matter.

acousticophobia: a fear of noise.

A HISTORY OF SOUND

How do we know all about sound? People have been wondering about sound since ancient times. Just as they looked up and questioned the stars and looked down and tried to understand the ocean, people have talked about and experimented with sound.

Ancient Greek thinker Pythagoras (c. 570–c. 495 BCE) was one of the first people to explore the concept of sound. He noticed that the length of a vibrating string affected the pitch or tone it produced. Aristotle (384 BCE–322 BCE), another ancient Greek, was one of the first to suggest that sound travels in waves. He did make a mistake when he theorized that high frequencies spread faster than lower frequencies—but that's okay! Science is built on mistakes and on the work done to correct those mistakes.

Pythagoras believed that music sounded beautiful because certain combinations of notes corresponded to special relationships between numbers. Scientists have proven this theory wrong, but Pythagoras should get credit for the thinking he did about sound!

Waving Molecules

What is it like to be a molecule in a sound wave? Stand in a circle with a group of friends. Everyone cross their arms in front of their chest. One person leans gently into the person beside them and then stands straight up again. That second person then leans gently into the next person and they lean into the next person and so on. Keep the wave going around the whole circle. What does it look like? Your group mimicked how molecules in a sound wave pass along energy. A molecule bumps against its neighbor, sending the energy along the wave. Scientists call this type of wave a longitudinal wave. Learn more about this type of wave in the "Modeling a Sound Wave" activity on page 32.

SUPER SOUND WAVES

It was Galileo Galilei (1564–1642), an Italian **physicist**, **engineer**, and **astronomer**, who really dove into studying sound vibrations. His father was a musician—maybe that's where his interest grew from. French mathematician Marin Mersenne (1588–1648) studied and wrote about vibrations and the speed at which they traveled through the air. He was also responsible for spreading the news about Galileo's work. Mersenne's book *Harmonicorum Libri* provided a foundation for modern musical **acoustics**.

> **Try a thought experiment to better understand how sound waves travel!** What conditions affect how a sound wave moves?
>
> 🔍 Branch Education speed of sound

Scientist Robert Boyle (1627–1691) and his assistant, Robert Hooke (1635–1703), conducted experiments in the mid-1600s to see if sound could travel through a **vacuum**. A vacuum is a space with little to no air molecules.

In one experiment, the scientists placed a ringing alarm clock under a jar. As they sucked the air out, the sound of the ring became softer. What do you think happened when the jar contained almost no air? The clock went silent!

People who fear noises have acousticophobia. For these people, loud noises can make them feel anxious or even physically sick. But there's treatment! Relaxation techniques, therapy, and medication often help.

17

THE SCIENCE OF SOUND

WORDS TO KNOW

Doppler effect: a change in the frequency of waves as an object changes position in relation to an observer.

microphone: a device that converts sound waves to electrical energy.

radio wave: a type of invisible wave used to transmit radio and television signals.

architectural acoustics: the science of designing a space to enhance sound within that space.

absorb: to soak up a liquid or take in energy, heat, light, or sound.

reflect: to bounce off a surface. To redirect something that hits a surface, such as heat, light, or sound.

innovation: a new invention or way of doing something.

It was Christian Doppler (1803–1853), an Austrian physicist, who came up with a mathematical equation to describe what happens when the source of a sound wave is moving. When a car passes you as you walk along a road, what happens? Does it sound the same the entire time you can see the car? No! Instead, the **Doppler effect** happens. The pitch is higher when the car is closer to you and lowers as the car moves away.

Sound vibrations do not travel directly between cell phones. A microphone changes the sound waves in our voice into electric signals, which turn into radio waves that travel to the other phone.

Have you ever seen a show in a concert hall? That hall was likely designed to produce the best sound possible. You can thank Wallace Sabine (1868–1919). He was an American physicist who founded the field of **architectural acoustics** when he was asked to help improve the acoustics of a museum. He began experimenting with different ways of **absorbing** and **reflecting** sound within a space.

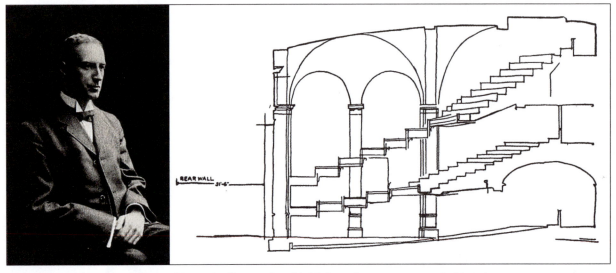

Wallace Sabine and a diagram from his "Collected papers on acoustics" (1922)

18

Doppler Effect

The siren on an ambulance is loud. Have you ever noticed that the pitch seems higher when the ambulance approaches and drops as it speeds away from you? When the ambulance approaches you, the sound waves are pushed closer together. You hear a higher pitch. What happens when the ambulance moves away? The sound waves are spread farther apart, and you hear a lower pitch. This is what makes the WEE-oww-WEE-oww sound. This is the Doppler effect. When we're out walking or driving, we instinctively use the Doppler effect to know where cars are coming from, which helps us stay safe.

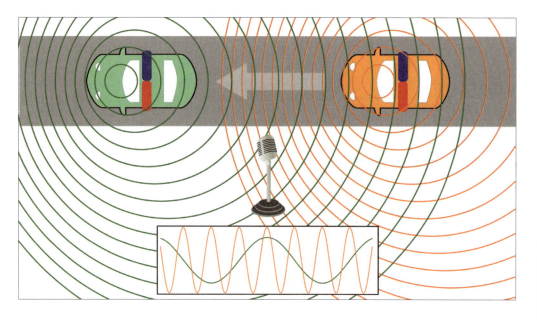

The work of scientists and researchers in the field of sound has produced some amazing results. As we learn more about sound waves and how they travel, and as our technology improves, we'll see new inventions and **innovations**.

One of the loudest sounds ever made on Earth happened more than 130 years ago. In 1883, Krakatoa, an island volcano in Indonesia, erupted. People heard the sound more than 3,000 miles away! You can hear a recording of the sound at this website.

🔍 Krakatoa sound

THE SCIENCE OF SOUND

WORDS TO KNOW

dissipate: to scatter in different directions and become less and less.

electromagnetic: magnetism developed with a current of electricity. Magnetism is a force caused by the motion of electrons that either attracts or repels objects.

HOW SOUND TRAVELS

In the Introduction, we talked about how sound needs a medium to travel through. Today, we know that sound travels through solids, liquids, and gases, but this conclusion was the result of a lot of scientific work.

The experiments done by Robert Boyle and Robert Hooke proved sound cannot travel through empty space. Sound waves can travel only through matter, such as a gas, a liquid, or a solid.

Plasma is another state of matter. Stars are made of plasma—in fact, there is more plasma in the universe than any other kind of matter. Can sound waves pass through plasma? Yes! Sound waves pass through plasma at a similar speed as they do through other gases.

How Do Phones Work?

You might think it's silly—two cans connected by a string being used as a telephone. But it works! When you talk into one can, your voice makes sound waves that vibrate the bottom of the can. Those vibrations travel along the string to the other can, transferring the sound of your voice. But the string has to be held taut for the sound waves to travel along it. This is similar to how landline telephones work. Those phones have a thin metal disk inside called a diaphragm that converts sound waves from your voice into electrical energy that travels over wires to another telephone, where that electrical energy is turned back into sound waves the other person can hear.

Cell phones work differently. In cell phones, a microphone turns your voice into an electrical signal, and then a microchip turns that signal into a radio wave that's beamed out through the phone's antenna to the closest cell tower. From there, the signal is passed to a base station that sorts where the call goes. When the call reaches its intended destination, the radio wave is changed back into an electrical signal and then into a sound wave so you can say "Hi" to your friend.

SUPER SOUND WAVES

Remember, matter is made up of molecules and sound travels by causing molecules to vibrate. Sound is energy that transfers from one molecule to another. As sound travels, its energy causes it to go wherever it can. Anywhere there's matter to move through, the sound will go. As sound waves travel farther from their source, they grow weaker. They spread out. Have you ever tossed a pebble in a pond? The ripples from the pebble start out strong, but by the time they get to the shore—if they get to the shore—they're much smaller. Sound waves work the same. As the sound energy touches more and more molecules, each individual molecule has less energy. The sound energy **dissipates**.

SOUND IN SPACE

Have you ever watched a science fiction movie that included a huge explosion deep in space, with lots of fire and loud noises? Filmmakers often get this wrong! Space is a vacuum—like the jars used by Boyle and Hooke in their experiments. Sound waves can't form in space because space contains no air molecules. How do astronauts on a spacewalk communicate with each other? Some types of waves, such as **electromagnetic** waves, can travel in space.

THE SCIENCE OF SOUND

> **WORDS TO KNOW**
>
> **International Space Station (ISS):** a massive space station orbiting Earth where astronauts live, conduct experiments, and study space.
>
> **electrolysis:** the process used to capture hydrogen from water using electricity.
>
> **solar panel:** a device used to capture sunlight and convert it to electrical energy.
>
> **echo:** a sound caused by the reflection of sound waves from a surface back to the speaker.

A radio wave is a type of electromagnetic wave. When astronauts work outside the **International Space Station (ISS)**, for example, microphones in their helmets pick up their voices and change the sound waves into radio waves.

Inside the ISS, there's plenty of oxygen for astronauts to breathe and to carry sound waves. Where does the oxygen come from?

Much of the oxygen inside the space station comes from a process called **electrolysis**, which uses electricity from the ISS **solar panels** to split water into oxygen and hydrogen.

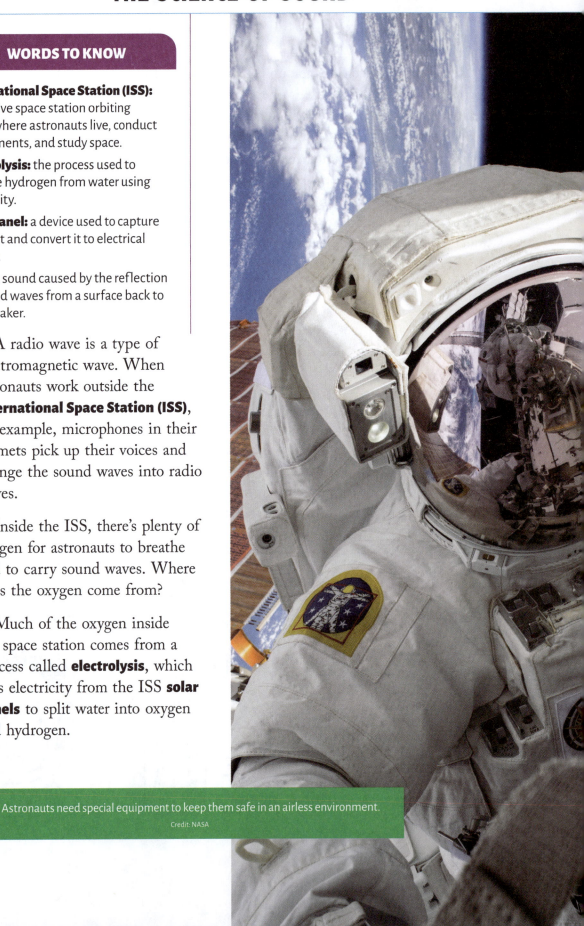

Astronauts need special equipment to keep them safe in an airless environment.
Credit: NASA

SUPER SOUND WAVES

Remember, a water molecule is made of two molecules of hydrogen and one of oxygen. When that molecule gets separated into its components, you've got some oxygen to breathe! You've also got air for sound waves to travel through.

ECHO, ECHO, ECHO

Now that we know more about how sound travels in waves through different mediums, let's look at what that means for using sound in everyday life.

Golconda, a 700-year-old fort in southeast India, is known for its acoustics. Arches built into the fort make sound waves travel far. The sound waves bounce back and forth between the ground and the arch. The sound of a clap underneath the fort's entrance, for example, can be heard more than half a mile away! Long ago, guards at the fort used handclaps to alert the army of attacking forces.

You don't have to travel to India to hear this sound effect. Try singing in the shower. *Do Re Mi!* Do you wonder why your voice sounds a little bouncy? What you're experiencing is the sound of an **echo**.

An echo is never as loud as the original sound. When a sound wave hits a hard surface, the surface absorbs some of the sound's energy.

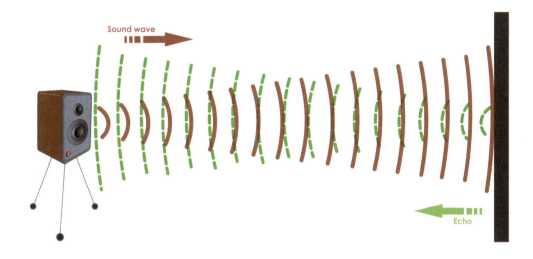

THE SCIENCE OF SOUND

WORDS TO KNOW

Hertz (Hz): a unit of frequency, equal to one cycle per second.

ultrasound imaging: a technique using sound waves that lets doctors see inside a body.

tissue: a large number of **cells** in an **organism** that are similar in form and function and grouped together, such as muscle tissue.

cell: the basic part of a living thing. Cells are so small they can be seen only with a microscope. There are billions of cells in most living things.

organism: a living thing, such as a plant or animal.

X-ray: radiation that allows doctors to see your bones.

radiation: electromagnetic energy transmitted in the form of rays, waves, or particles from a source, such as the sun.

Sound waves bounce off hard surfaces. What happens when you throw a rubber ball against the pavement? The rubber ball bounces, doesn't it? Sound waves also bounce, creating an echo when they hit a hard surface, such as stone arches or the walls of a shower.

A tomb built in 1852 has one of the longest echoes in the world. At the Hamilton Mausoleum in Glasgow, Scotland, visitors can hear their voices echo for an amazing 15 seconds! The tomb once held the Guinness Book world record for the longest echo.

We measure frequency in Hertz (Hz), named after Heinrich Hertz (1857–1894). In the 1880s, the German scientist discovered how to send and receive radio waves.

In 2014, an acoustics professor broke the record when he fired blanks from a gun into an underground tunnel. That echo didn't fade for 112 seconds!

Echoes are an essential part of medicine. Using a technique called **ultrasound imaging**, doctors use echoes to take pictures of different parts of the human body. An ultrasound probe, about the size of a bar of soap, is attached to a computer. A doctor or technician moves the probe over the patient's body. The probe sends ultrasound waves into the patient's body, where they bounce off **tissues** back to the probe. Based on the time it takes for the echo to return, the computer builds a two-dimensional image of the part of the body being examined. Some newer ultrasound machines use computer software to create three-dimensional images.

Check out this video to witness the Hamilton Mausoleum echo. How does the musician use the echo to enhance the music he's playing?

🔎 Hamilton Mausoleum Tommy Smith

SUPER SOUND WAVES

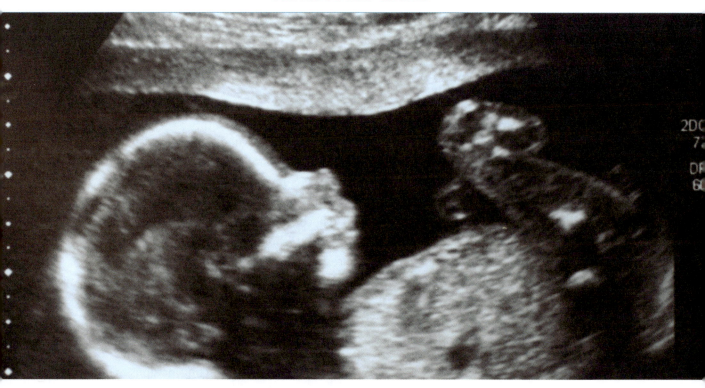

An ultrasound image of a baby inside its mother

One use for ultrasound is to check on the health of an unborn baby. Doctors also use ultrasound to study organs and the blood flow to a patient's heart.

This technique is different from using **X-rays**. X-rays use a kind of electromagnetic wave called **radiation** to peek inside the body, while ultrasounds use sound waves. Ultrasounds are good for viewing soft tissues, such as muscles and organs, while X-rays are useful with bones and dense tissue.

How does ultrasound work? Learn more in this video! How did scientists use their knowledge about bats to develop technology that could help human babies before they're born?

TED-Ed Jacques Abramowicz sound

Ultrasound produces sound waves that vibrate more than 20,000 times per second! That measurement is more than 20,000 Hz. That's a little higher than human ears can hear. People can detect sound frequencies between about 20 Hz and almost 20,000 Hz.

THE SCIENCE OF SOUND

WORDS TO KNOW

magnetic resonance imaging (MRI): a form of medical imaging that uses high-frequency radio waves and a strong magnetic field.

echolocation: the ability to find an object by sending out sound waves and listening for them to bounce back.

sonar: a method of using sound pulses to detect objects and to measure the depth of water.

prey: an animal hunted and eaten by other animals.

ECHOLOCATION

Another way we use bouncing sound waves is for **echolocation**—and we're not the only ones! How do bats fly around at night and avoid hitting trees, buildings, and other bats? Echolocation.

Bats emit high-frequency sound waves through their mouth or nose and then listen as those sound waves bounce off everything in the bat's environment, letting it maneuver around obstacles in the dark.

This same concept is at work in **sonar** systems used to explore the ocean floor.

Career Connection

A radiologist is a medical doctor with a specialty in using medical imaging techniques such as X-rays, ultrasounds, **magnetic resonance imaging (MRI)**, and more. To become a radiologist, you need to go to medical school and complete a four-year residency, plus undergo specialized training.

There are different kinds of radiologists.

› Interventional radiologists diagnose and treat patients who might have heart disease, stroke, or cancer by guiding instruments through tiny incisions to reach the area that needs treatment. They use X-rays and MRI to help "see" inside the body.

› Diagnostic radiologists use many different imaging techniques to diagnose someone's condition.

› Radiation oncologists oversee treatments for cancer patients.

All of the imaging techniques use different kinds of waves to provide a road map of a patient's body.

SUPER SOUND WAVES

Instead of diving to dangerous depths to see what's down there, scientists can direct sound waves down through the water and use sensors to show the outline of that watery world.

We'll learn more about both of these phenomena later in the book.

Now that we've looked at sound waves, let's learn how we hear a sound. We will also learn how our hearing compares to that of animals. Will it be much different from how we listen? Let's find out!

ESSENTIAL QUESTION

Why do sounds get fainter as you travel farther from the source?

TEXT TO WORLD

Do you have pets? Do you think they use sound the same way humans do?

Animals use their hearing to communicate, locate **prey**, and detect danger. This fox is likely using its hearing to find some lunch under the snow!

STRING TELEPHONE

TOOL KIT
- science notebook and pencil
- pushpin
- 2 paper cups
- waxed dental floss
- 2 paper clips

What if you had only paper cups and dental floss to make a telephone? You might think, "No one is going to hear me!" Let's see if you can make a paper cup ring! Do this activity with a partner.

> **Use the pushpin to poke a hole in the bottom of each cup.**

> **Cut a piece of dental floss approximately 10 feet long.** Thread the ends of the dental floss through the holes at the bottom of each cup and secure each end with a paper clip.

Method	Prediction	Result
Loose floss		
Taut floss		
Pinched floss		

> **Start a scientific method worksheet in your science notebook.** What is your hypothesis? What do you think will happen when you talk into a cup? Organize your experiment in a chart.

> **Give one cup to a partner.** Keep the floss loose and talk into the cup. Can you hear each other?

> **Stretch the floss tight.** Predict what will happen to the sound. Speak into the cup again. Was your prediction correct?

> **Repeat the experiment but pinch the floss when you talk.** How will pinching the floss affect your results? Write down a prediction in your science notebook.

> **Record your observations in your science notebook and answer these questions.** When were you able to hear your partner? How did the sound of your voice travel?

WHAT'S HAPPENING?

In the experiment, the cup vibrates when you speak. These vibrations move along the floss to your partner's ear. When the floss is taut, it vibrates faster and the sound becomes clearer. The sound does not travel through the pinched floss.

Try This!

How would the experiment change if you used a piece of yarn? A thin chain? Try and see. Which material is best at transmitting waves?

CONDUCTING SOUND

What happens to the sounds we hear when they travel in the air and underwater? Do they sound the same or is one louder? Let's find out in this project! Have a partner help you with part of this.

> **Cut the end from the balloon and pull it over the end of one funnel.** Hold it in place with duct tape.

> **Push one end of the tubing over the spout of the funnel.** Do the same at the other end with the second funnel. You may need tape to hold the tubing in place.

> **Place the funnel with the balloon against your chest.** Hold the other funnel to your ear. Does the tubing conduct sound? Write down your observations.

> **As you listen with the funnel, ask a partner to hit the two metal spoons together in the air.** Make a prediction. What do you hear? Write your observations in your notebook.

> **What will happen if you repeat the spoon experiment underwater?** Make a prediction.

> **Fill the pail three-quarters full of water.** Place the balloon funnel in the water and the other end to your ear. Have your partner strike the spoons underwater. Was your prediction correct? Write down all your observations.

TOOL KIT
- balloon
- scissors
- 2 plastic funnels (or DIY from the tops of 2 two-liter bottles)
- duct tape
- 2½ feet of flexible tubing (diameter needs to be slightly wider than the funnel spout)
- 2 metal spoons
- large plastic pail
- science notebook and pencil

Try This!
Can your funnel work against a solid? Hold the balloon end against a wall and have a partner tap the spoon. What do you hear? Have them tap farther away. Does the sound change?

WHAT'S HAPPENING?
Did the spoons sound different in the air than underwater? If so, why do you think this was? Water is a better conductor of sound than air because water molecules are packed closer together than air molecules.

STETHOSCOPE SCIENCE

Stethoscopes help doctors hear sounds within the body. Let's investigate how this instrument works. What will you hear? Have a partner assist you.

TOOL KIT
- scissors
- string
- metal coat hanger, plastic hanger
- metal spoon
- science notebook and pencil

➤ **Make the stethoscope tubes by cutting two 20-inch lengths of string.** Tie one end of the string to each corner of the wire hanger.

➤ **Wind the end of each string around your pointer fingers and hold your fingers to your ears.**

➤ **Allow the hanger to swing freely.** Have a partner tap on the hanger with the spoon. Can you hear the tapping? Record your observations in your science notebook.

WHAT'S HAPPENING?
The sounds we hear with a stethoscope run from the chest piece through tubes to the ears. The tubes conduct sound, and therefore we hear it.

René Laennec (1781–1826) invented the stethoscope in 1816. The French doctor experimented with instruments that would help him listen to his patients' chests. He rolled paper into a funnel and built stethoscopes out of wood and ivory. He found a simple, wooden tube worked best.

Check out images of early stethoscopes on this website. How do they differ from your stethoscope? How do they differ from the stethoscopes doctors use today?

🔍 past medical history stethoscope

Try This!

How will the sound change if you use a plastic or a wooden hanger? Try and see. Compare your results with the first experiment.

SEEING SOUND WAVES

> **TOOL KIT**
> - pot or bowl
> - plastic wrap
> - dry rice
> - cookie sheet or baking pan
> - metal spoon

Sound waves start at a source that vibrates. The vibrating source causes the medium—usually air—around it to also vibrate. These vibrating particles create waves that travel from the sound's source invisibly through the air. When sound waves reach your ear, your eardrum vibrates as part of the hearing process. In this experiment, you'll be able to "see" how sound travels and how these waves affect the eardrum.

Musician Francis Macdonald recorded a piece of music written to be played in a space with a long echo. You can listen to it at this website. How might it sound played in a place with no echo? What does the echo add to the music?

ClassicFM Hamilton Mausoleum

▶ **Stretch some plastic wrap tightly across the open end of a pot or bowl.** The opening should be covered completely and be smooth.

▶ **Place about 1 tablespoon of dry rice on top of the plastic wrap.**

▶ **Hold a metal cookie sheet or baking pan near the bowl with the plastic wrap but make sure it does not touch the bowl.** What do you think will happen when you make a loud noise? Why?

▶ **Test your prediction.** Using a metal spoon, bang the sheet or pan loudly.

✳ What happens to the dry rice? How do you explain what you observed? Was your prediction right? Why or why not?

▶ **Vary the volume of the noise you are producing by changing how hard you bang on the sheet or pan.** What effect does this have on the rice?

✳ How do you explain what you observe?

✳ How does this experiment mimic how an eardrum reacts to a sound?

Try This!

Test other noises at different volumes and observe what happens to the rice each time. What do you observe? What conclusions can you make based on your observations?

MODELING A
SOUND WAVE

Sound waves are invisible, but they are part of every moment of our lives. Let's use a spring toy to model how sound travels. Have a partner help you.

> **TOOL KIT**
> - plastic spring toy, such as a Slinky
> - 2 hand weights (you can use textbooks)
> - string
> - scissors
> - science notebook and pencil

▶ **Place the spring and the weights on a table.**

▶ **Tie a piece of string to one end of the spring and a weight.** Repeat with another piece of string on the other end of the spring and the other weight.

▶ **Have a partner hold on to one weight while you hold on to the other.** Stretch out the coil. It shouldn't be too rigid.

▶ **Place one hand at each end of the spring.** Push rhythmically on one end of the spring toy to create a compression wave. Do this several times, trying different rhythms.

▶ **What do you notice about each loop after the wave passes?** Record your observations.

WHAT'S HAPPENING?

Each loop represents an air molecule. As the energy in a sound wave moves, some molecules press together, while others are spread apart like the rippling coils of the spring. This wave is called a longitudinal wave. The vibration moves parallel to the direction that the sound wave moves.

Try This!

Sound waves spread out in all directions like water ripples. Fill a large glass mixing bowl three-quarters full of water. Drop a pebble into the center of the bowl. Do you notice the water ripples spread out? What happens to them?

Chapter 2

HEROIC
HEARING

Baseball mitts catch balls. Winter mittens catch snowballs. Do you know what else catches things? Your ears! The human ear captures sound waves the same as mitts catch balls. How?

ESSENTIAL QUESTION

How does the shape of a creature's ear affect how it hears?

The five basic **senses** are sight, smell, taste, touch, and hearing. Our senses have an essential job. They gather information. They tell us what's going on around us. Our sense of hearing, for example, tells us if a sound is a dog barking—woof—or a car honking—beep. How exactly does our hearing work?

WORDS TO KNOW

senses: sight, smell, taste, touch, and hearing are the five senses, all of which give a living thing the ability to learn about its surroundings.

THE SCIENCE OF SOUND

WORDS TO KNOW

pinna: the outer ear in humans and other **mammals**.

mammal: a type of animal, such as a human, dog, or cat. Mammals are born live, feed milk to their young, and usually have hair or fur covering most of their skin.

ear canal: a passage that connects the outer ear to the eardrum.

eardrum: a thin membrane in the middle ear that vibrates in response to sound waves.

tympanic membrane: the scientific term for the eardrum.

ossicles: three small bones in the middle ear that vibrate in response to sound waves.

stapes: found in the middle ear, the smallest bone in the human body.

cochlea: the part of the ear where sound waves are turned into electrical signals and sent to the brain for hearing.

brain stem: the lower part of the brain that connects to the spinal cord.

thalamus: a part of the brain that acts as a relay station for sensory information.

neuron: a single nerve cell that carries messages between the brain and other parts of the body.

harmony: a pleasing blend of sounds.

rhythm: a regular beat in music.

> Look at this cartoon video and get a tour of the inside of your ear! How do the three parts of the ear work together?
>
> 🔎 KidsHealth ear

JOURNEY INSIDE THE EAR

Our ears let us hear. The average adult ear is about 2½ inches long. The ear might not be big, but it's a powerful microphone that picks up sounds around us. See the chart of sound heard by humans in Chapter 4 to get a better idea of all the work the ear does.

The three main parts of the human ear are the outer ear, middle ear, and inner ear. They work together with the brain to make sense of sound waves. Sound waves strike the outer ear first. The outer ear is the part of our ear that we can see. The outer ear includes the lobes, or the **pinna**.

The inner ear grows during our entire life!

The outer ear directs sound waves into the **ear canal**, where they travel to the **eardrum**, or the **tympanic membrane**.

The membrane is a thin piece of skin that separates the ear canal from the middle ear. Inside the middle ear are three tiny bones. They are called the **ossicles**. These small bones fit on top of a penny! The **stapes** is one of the three ossicle bones in the middle ear and is the smallest bone in the human body. The incus and the malleus are the other ossicle bones.

HEROIC HEARING

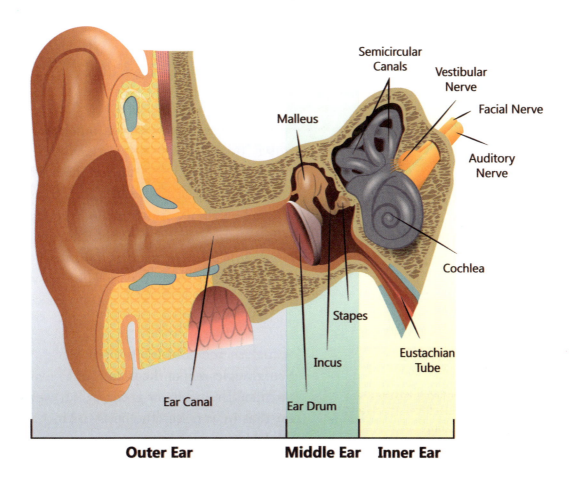

The ossicles pass the sound waves to the inner ear, where the **cochlea** is. The cochlea is a tiny, pea-sized organ filled with fluid. It resembles a snail shell. Sound waves cause the fluid to ripple. Thousands of hair cells also line the cochlea. When the hair cells vibrate, small electrical signals travel to the brain.

The middle ear is less than a half inch in size.

Inside the brain, the **brain stem** and **thalamus** use those electric signals to understand where the sound is coming from. Inside another part of the brain, the primary auditory cortex, different **neurons** interpret frequency, intensity, duration, **harmony**, **rhythm**, and more.

THE SCIENCE OF SOUND

WORDS TO KNOW

impaired: weakened or damaged.

deaf: having total or partial hearing loss.

genetic: traits that are passed from parent to child in DNA.

hearing aid: a small device that fits in or on the ear, worn by a partially deaf person to amplify sound.

audiologist: a healthcare professional who treats hearing disorders. Audio relates to sound.

ear trumpet: a funnel-shaped device that collects sound waves and leads them into the ear.

vacuum tube: an electronic device that controls the flow of electrons in a vacuum.

transmitter: a device that sends out radio or television signals.

transistor: a device that controls the flow of electricity.

SOUND AND THE HEARING IMPAIRED

Some people are born hearing **impaired** or **deaf**. This can happen because of an infection in either the mother or the baby, premature birth, or other illnesses. Deafness can also be **genetic**. Many people lose their hearing as they get older, either through natural aging, illness, damage to the ear, or from working for long periods in noisy environments, such as a factory or a concert venue.

Children and adults with damaged hearing might rely on **hearing aids** to make sounds louder and more precise. They wear these aids in or behind their ears. An **audiologist** fits the aids to make sure they are comfortable and work well.

The Shape of Your Ear

The shape of the ear affects how we hear. Touch your outer ear. How would you describe its shape? The outer ear points forward. So, human ears collect more sounds from the front than from behind. What about horses? Horses can move their ears to point in different directions, front to back. When they sense danger in front of them, they point their ears fully toward the front to learn as much as possible about what might be coming from that direction. When there's something rustling behind them, they rotate their ears toward the back of their bodies to better know when it's time to run from danger. Dogs, too, move their outer ears to get a better sense of where a sound is coming from. They have at least 18 muscles working hard to hear!

HEROIC HEARING

Hearing devices have been around for a very long time. The **ear trumpet** was officially recognized as a hearing aid device in 1634. It worked like this: The small end of the horn went into the ear canal while the wider end of the horn jutted out to catch sound waves. This amplified the sound for the user.

In 1895, the first electric hearing aid was invented by American engineer Miller Reese Hutchinson (1876–1944). He called it the akouphone. This was a portable electric device that was much bulkier than what we have today. But for people suffering from hearing loss, it was a game changer. During the 1920s and 1930s, **vacuum tube** hearing aids were popular. These used telephone **transmitters** to turn speech into electrical signals, which were then amplified with a receiver so the user could better hear the sound. When **transistors** were developed in 1948, hearing aids took advantage of this leap in technology by becoming smaller and more portable.

A collapsible Victorian ear trumpet made of tin

Credit: Wellcome Images (CC BY 4.0)

THE SCIENCE OF SOUND

WORDS TO KNOW

amplifier: an electronic device that increases the strength or power of sounds.

speaker: a device designed to change electrical signals into sound waves that can be heard.

cochlear implant: an electronic device to help people with hearing loss to recognize some sounds.

electrode: a conductor through which electricity enters and leaves an object such as a battery.

In 1956, behind-the-ear hearing aids were developed, which were far more comfortable and easier to use than the akouphone, and by the 1970s, in-the-ear hearing aids were proving even more effective. Digital technology in the 1990s and early 2000s improved hearing aids even more, and now that we have Bluetooth technology, people with hearing challenges have many options for listening to the world.

Hair cells in the cochlea are similar to piano keys. Each hair cell reacts to a different pitch.

A hearing aid has three essential parts. A microphone picks up sound. It converts sound waves into electrical signals that travel to an **amplifier**. The amplifier makes the signals louder. Hair cells in the ear detect loud sound vibrations more easily. The signals move on to the ear through a **speaker**.

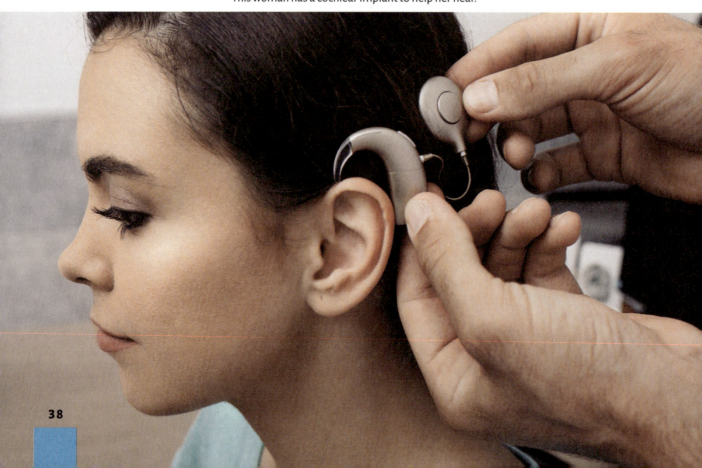

This woman has a cochlear implant to help her hear.

HEROIC HEARING

Some hearing aids, such as a **cochlear implant**, use a computer chip. A cochlear implant is a small electronic device that helps people who have severely damaged hearing. People who have complete deafness, however, cannot use a cochlear implant.

Surgeons place part of the cochlear implant under the skin and behind the ear. Sound waves enter a microphone behind the ear. From here, they travel to a tiny computer that processes the information. The information travels from outside to inside the ear through a wire. **Electrodes** inside the cochlea send these signals to the brain, which the brain interprets as sounds. These electrodes take the place of the hair cells in the cochlea. It is damage or lack of hair cells that usually leads to hearing loss, since they are delicate and easily damaged by loud noises, head trauma, or infection.

It can take a lot of practice to learn how to understand those electrical signals as sound—it's not like flicking a switch. Often, people also use other forms of communication, such as lip reading and sign language, even if they have a cochlear implant.

Can elephants hear the rain before it falls? Find out in this video! How might this ability have helped the species survive?

🔎 BBC elephant infrasound

Artificial Ear

In 2013, doctors and engineers at Cornell University used a 3-D printer and ear tissue from a cow to create an artificial ear. They began the process by printing a plastic model of an ear and then filling that model with collagen, which is a kind of protein. Then, they introduced cartilage cells—taken from a cow—into the collagen. Those cells began to reproduce and eventually replaced the collagen. In 2022, doctors created an ear made from the patient's own cells and transplanted that ear onto the patient's head. Eventually, ears made from living tissue could provide a realistic option for people.

Watch this video about how scientists grew an ear in a laboratory. What other things might they be able to create that would help people?

🔎 3D printer ear AP

THE SCIENCE OF SOUND

> **WORDS TO KNOW**
>
> **navigate:** to find the way from one place to another.
>
> **GPS:** Global Positioning System, a device that determines its location on Earth using signals sent from different **satellites** in space.
>
> **satellite:** a manmade object placed into orbit around Earth, often carrying instruments to gather data.
>
> **beacon:** a device that sends out a signal indicating location.

SOUND AND INDEPENDENCE

Some people use sound in ways that might surprise you. Our world is mostly created by people who see and hear within similar ranges, but for people outside those ranges, this can pose a challenge. Sound is one way those people rise to the challenge.

Have you ever seen a visually impaired person using a cane to help them **navigate** their path? A support cane helps them travel more efficiently. Tap tap tap. They sweep the cane back and forth to find and avoid them obstacles.

Career Connection

When a child or adult has trouble communicating, they'll often see a speech language pathologist (SLP) for help. Also called a speech therapist, an SLP can help people learn how to form sounds and speak easily so that others can understand them. They might suggest exercises to strengthen the muscles used to speak or swallow. An SLP also teaches people how to use different forms of communication when speech doesn't work for them, so they can more easily operate in a world that requires communication.

SLPs can work with people on how their voice sounds, how loudly or softly they talk, stuttering, organizing, sucking and chewing habits, and many other issues. There are several different types of speech therapy, including articulation therapy that helps people make their speech more clear, language intervention therapy for people with speech delays, and modeling techniques. People who benefit from speech therapy can be as young as toddlers or quite elderly—there's no age limit!

HEROIC HEARING

Newer canes are high tech. They have **GPS** locators and sensors that vibrate when they sense an obstacle.

Echoes also help the visually impaired. As we learned in Chapter 1, echoes are sound waves that bounce off objects. Some animals use these sound waves to learn more about their environment in a technique called echolocation. It turns out, certain people have that ability!

Hearing and Seeing

Sound technology helps the visually impaired navigate unfamiliar areas, including subways. One navigation system uses a smartphone app and **beacons** within subways to figure out where someone is. The beacons send messages to a smartphone the visually impaired person listens to with headphones.

In 2022, Leslie Hodgson became the oldest person to receive a cochlear implant—at age 103!

Remember, echolocation is when an organism uses sound waves to detect their environment. Just as people with average sight abilities use light waves to detect the world around them, others use sound waves to figure out their surroundings.

Daniel Kish (1966–), the president of World Access for the Blind, is an expert at using echolocation to walk, run, ride a bike, and keep a picture in his mind of his surroundings.

Blind since he was a child, he learned at a young age that he didn't need sight to live fully in the world.

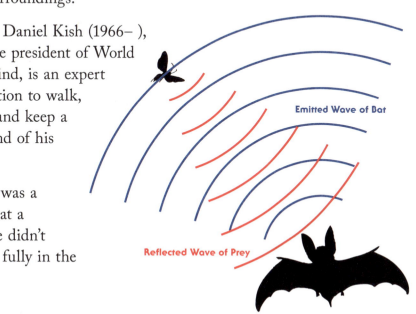

THE SCIENCE OF SOUND

WORDS TO KNOW

insect: an animal that has three body parts and six legs and its skeleton on the outside of its body. Many insects have wings. Grasshoppers, ants, ladybugs, and honeybees are insects.

evolve: to change or develop slowly, during long periods of time.

predator: an animal that hunts and eats other animals.

auditory: relating to hearing.

oscilloscope: a device that shows the movement of sound waves.

Kish's technique is similar to how bats fly at night. Bats make high-frequency sounds to detect where they are in the dark and to discover and chase their prey.

Too much sound or too little sound or sounds that are too high or too low to hear can cause problems for everyone. Still, people and animals need sound to communicate, and sound is a very efficient way of doing just that. We'll learn more about sound and communication in the next chapter.

Insect Ears

Lacewings have ears on their wings, some moths have ears on their mouths, and bladder grasshoppers have six pairs of ears on their abdomens! **Insects** have been **evolving** for about 480 million years, so it makes sense they have lots of different types of ears. After all, they need to hear the prey they want to catch or the **predator** that's coming for them. Some insects hear very well. A male mosquito has about 15,000 neurons that are used for hearing, making it very sensitive to sound, but some moths have only one or two neurons working on the sound board. Humans generally have a little more than 30,000 **auditory** neurons!

ESSENTIAL QUESTION

How does the shape of a creature's ear affect how it hears?

TEXT TO WORLD

Are you or anyone you know hearing impaired? What are some ways you or they adjust?

EXPLORE SOUND WITH A
HOMEMADE GUITAR

A guitar uses strings to make sound and music. In this activity, you'll make a homemade guitar from common household materials and explore how this instrument produces sound.

> **TOOL KIT**
> - shoebox
> - variety of rubber bands of different lengths and widths but long enough to fit over a shoebox
> - paper towel roll
> - tape

▸ **Take a shoebox or other rectangular container and cut an opening in the top or take the lid off completely.**

▸ **Stretch at least four different rubber bands over the box around its long end.** Try to pick ones that have different lengths or widths. Space them evenly across the open space of the box.

▸ **Tape one end of a paper towel roll to one of the shorter sides of the rectangular box.** It should stick out from the box like a guitar neck.

Frequency is the number of vibrations produced by a moving object in one second. Faster frequencies produce higher sounds. Lower frequencies produce lower sounds.

▸ **Experiment making sound with the guitar.** Strum and pluck the different bands on the guitar.

✱ Which one makes the lowest sound?

✱ Which makes the highest sound?

✱ Can you explain why the different rubber bands make different sounds?

▸ **Try to re-order the bands on the guitar so they play notes from lowest to highest.** What type of rubber bands work best?

Try This!

To investigate more, check out an online virtual **oscilloscope** to "see" the sound waves produced by your guitar. An oscilloscope gives a visual picture of a sound's waveform.

🔍 virtual oscilloscope

43

VIBRATING DRUM

Our ears detect sounds because of vibrations. Let's model how sound waves cause the eardrum to vibrate by using wax paper, a bowl, salt, and energy provided by you!

> **Start a scientific method worksheet in your science notebook.** What is your hypothesis? How will sound affect the salt?

> **Cut out a piece of wax paper larger than the diameter of the bowl.** Cover the bowl with the paper and hold it in place with the rubber band. Measure and pour 1 tablespoon of salt over the wax paper. Does the salt move?

> **Lean over the wax paper and clap your hands softly.** Record your observations.

> **Clap your hands loudly and write down your observations.** Compare your results.

WHAT'S HAPPENING?
Which method moved the salt the most? Which sound do you think would make your ear vibrate the most and why? A loud clap creates more sound energy with larger vibrations than a quieter clap. A loud sound will make the eardrum vibrate more.

TOOL KIT
- science notebook and pencil
- scissors
- wax paper or plastic wrap
- small glass bowl
- rubber band
- measuring spoons
- salt

Try This!
Make more sounds over your drum, such as banging a pot over the wax paper. How do the results change?

Say What?
As people age, they lose hair cells in the cochlea. Older adults often lose their ability to hear higher-pitched sounds first. Do you know any older adults who have trouble hearing? From the mid-2000s, a security company used this information to create a sound only teenagers could detect. Businesses used this sound to stop teenagers from hanging around places where they had no reason to be. However, some teenagers decided to use the high-pitched sound to their advantage. They turned the sound into a cell phone ringtone, called the mosquito ringtone, that only they could hear. They could receive messages in class, and their teachers wouldn't know!

WHERE'S THAT SOUND?

Our ears catch sound waves. Do you need both your ears to figure out where a sound is? Do some investigating and find out. You will need a partner for this activity.

> **Place the sound makers on the tray.** Cover your eyes with the blindfold and place an earmuff over or ear plug in one ear.

> **Ask your partner to make a sound with one object at a time from the left, right, behind, and in front of you.** Record what you hear at each point.

> **Remove the earmuff and repeat the steps.** Is it easier to pick up the sounds with one ear or both?

WHAT'S HAPPENING?
Your brain receives information from sound waves from both ears. This is called **stereophonic hearing**. When a person uses only one ear, the brain's job is more difficult. Did your results show this? If not, why do you think this was?

> **TOOL KIT**
> - assorted sound makers
> - tray
> - blindfold
> - earmuffs or ear plugs
> - partner
> - science notebook and pencil

Loud sounds make the hair cells in the ear bend more than quiet sounds. Not unlike blades of grass, the hairs will straighten after some time.

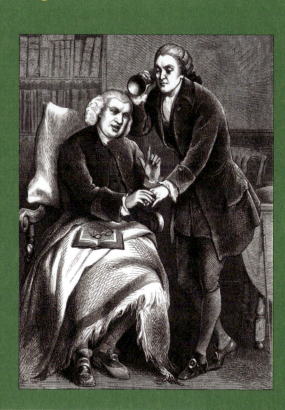

Try This!

Do the experiment again but use paper funnels to listen to the sounds. How do the funnels help you figure out the location of the sounds?

WORDS TO KNOW

stereophonic hearing: a way of reproducing sound using more than one microphone so the experience is similar to hearing it live.

ANIMAL EARS

Just like humans, animals detect sounds. Animal ears come in many different shapes. In this activity, you'll design, construct, and test three different ear shapes. Which of your designs will help you hear sounds more clearly? You will need a partner for this activity.

> **TOOL KIT**
> - scissors
> - construction paper
> - tape
> - scientific notebook and pencil
> - tissue paper

▶ **Cut out two large squares from the construction paper and fold each piece into a funnel and tape the seam closed.** Hold the smaller end of the funnels to your ears and have your partner make a sound. Record your observations in your notebook.

▶ **Make the funnels smaller or larger.** Repeat the sound and see if your results change.

Moths have the best hearing of any creature in the world. The great wax moth, for example, has extraordinary hearing. While the human ear hears sounds only up to 20 kHz, the great wax moth can hear sounds up to 300 kHz! Watch this video to learn some amazing facts about moths! Do you see moths where you live?

🔎 GeoBeats moths Dailymotion

THINK MORE!

Cut out a pair of full and floppy elephant-inspired ears from the tissue paper. Repeat the sound and compare your results. Which set of ears helped you to hear better and why? Which set helped you the least and why? Many animals move their ears in the direction of a sound. Try moving your paper ear models. Does it make a difference?

Strange Ears

Snakes feel sounds through an inner ear connected to their jawbone. The jawbone rests on the ground as a snake slithers around. Sound travels through the ground to the snake's jawbone and inner ear. A signal races to the snake's brain, and it wriggles to safety.

Scientists believe dolphins are another species that uses its jawbone to hear. Dolphins have some of the best hearing among organisms—they can hear far more frequencies than humans. Like snakes, no ears jut out from their heads, but they do have one small opening on each side that helps them know where sound is coming from under water.

HEARING FROM A DISTANCE

TOOL KIT
- science notebook and pencil
- paper, coin, smartphone
- sticky notes
- measuring tape

Elephants can communicate with other elephants miles away. Human ears aren't that sensitive. In this activity, discover how far away you hear certain sounds. You'll want to perform this experiment in a space with a hard floor and no carpet. You will also need a partner for this activity.

▶ **Start a scientific method worksheet in your science notebook.** How far away will you be able to hear paper crumpling, a coin drop, and a phone ringing quietly? What is your hypothesis? Which sound will be the easiest to hear from farthest away? Organize your experiment in a chart.

▶ **Ask your partner to crumple some paper (and keep crumpling it).** What do you think will happen when you walk away from the sound of crumpling paper? Slowly walk away until you don't hear the paper. Mark this spot with a sticky note. Take the measuring tape, measure the distance between the paper and the sticky note, and write this number down in your science notebook.

Listen to Daniel Kish's TED talk in this video. How is Kish's experience of the world different from yours? How is it similar?

🔍 Daniel Kish TED

▶ **What will happen if you do the same experiment again but drop a coin instead?** Write down your hypothesis in your science notebook. Ask your partner to drop the coin repeatedly. Mark the spot where you can no longer hear it and measure the distance. Write down your observations.

▶ **Predict what will happen if you use the ring of a smartphone at a quiet volume.** Ask your partner to call the phone, mark the spot where you can no longer hear the ring, and then measure the distance.

▶ **Compare your results with your predictions.** Which object could you hear farthest away? Which object could you hardly hear? Why do you think this was?

Try This!

Change places with your partner, repeat the activity, and compare the results. If a television played in the background, would your results change? Try it and see.

47

Chapter 3

PITCH
PERFECT

A class of 20 children shuffle across the stage to get in place for their concert. Everyone shushes. Voices soar and rumble. Hey, did someone *squeak*? Why doesn't everyone sound the same? After all, everyone practiced the same songs all week. Did they forget the music?

No. It's the way the human voice is made! We all sound different. Just as we all look different and move differently and think differently, our voices are different. Let's learn more.

ESSENTIAL QUESTION

How do different creatures make different sounds?

Vocal cords can vibrate as much as 1,000 times per second when you sing! The higher the note, the faster the vocal cords vibrate.

PITCH PERFECT

BOX IT UP

Humans have a voice box, or **larynx**. It's not an actual box. The larynx is an organ that sits on top of a tube called the **windpipe**. This tube runs from the nose and mouth to the lungs. We use our larynx to speak, laugh, shout, and sing.

The larynx has another important job. It also acts as a door. When we swallow, it's the larynx that stops food from traveling down the **trachea** into our lungs.

Two thin bands of muscle called **vocal cords** are attached to the walls of the larynx. When we breathe in, the vocal cords stay close together. When we breathe out, air flows from our lungs past the vocal cords, making them vibrate.

Vocal cords can vibrate hundreds of times per second! When the vibrations reach our mouth, the cheeks, lips, and tongue shape the noise into different sounds. These movements are how we speak or make buzzing, mumbling, grunting, and other sounds.

WORDS TO KNOW

larynx: also known as the voice box, an organ that sits in the neck.

windpipe: also known as the trachea, a tube that runs from the nose and mouth to the lungs.

trachea: the windpipe, the tube through which air enters the lungs.

vocal cord: one of two thin bands of muscle stretched across the larynx through which air passes in the process of making sound.

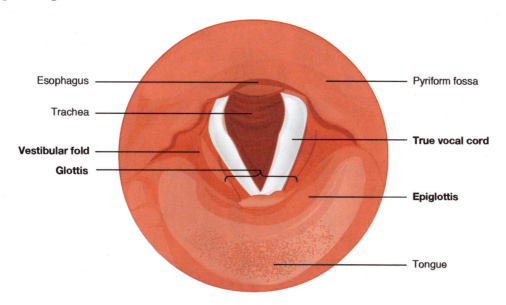

Inside the larynx
Credit: Betts et al., 2013 (CC BY 4.0)

THE SCIENCE OF SOUND

WORDS TO KNOW

hormone: a chemical that carries signals from one part of the body to another.

Inuit: a group of **indigenous** peoples who live in northern Canada, parts of Greenland, and Alaska.

indigenous: describes people who are native to a place.

duet: when two people sing together.

YOUR UNIQUE SOUND

Sing a note. Now, look at your fingertips. Do you notice any similarities? Probably not! But, in fact, your voice is as unique as your fingerprints. The sound of your voice depends on the shape and size of your mouth, larynx, and vocal cords. Your age and gender influence your voice, too.

How are the voices of males and females different? When men speak, their voices are usually lower than women's. This is because men typically have longer vocal cords than women. Long vocal cords vibrate at a lower frequency than short vocal cords. So, the frequency of a male voice is usually lower than that of a female's voice.

How are the voices in your family similar and how are they unique?

How might this choir sound different from a choir of children?

PITCH PERFECT

Family Tones

You might share certain traits—such as hair color, nose shape, and height—with family members. Your voices might be similar, too. The size and shape of your vocal cords are determined by genetics, just like everything else in your body. Do a little test and record the voices of friends or family members. How is each voice unique? Do they share any similar qualities?

Young peoples' vocal cords are still growing. Compared to an adult's, their vocal cords are much smaller and thinner. But, as children mature and their vocal cords grow with their bodies, their voices change. For example, boys' voices deepen as they age because their vocal cords grow longer and thicken. Girls' vocal cords also change but not as much as boys. Have you noticed your voice change as you've grown older?

Hormones are another thing that affect a person's voice. As people go through puberty or if they undergo hormone treatment, those new hormones can change the form of the larynx and vocal chords, making the person's voice deeper or higher.

Voice also depends on a person's health. Have you ever been asked if you have a frog in your throat? *Croak!* You probably didn't have an actual frog in your throat, but maybe you had a cold that left your vocal cords swollen. That makes your voice sound hoarse.

Many Inuit live in communities in northern Canada. The Inuit have a special singing tradition. Some Inuit practice a vocal game known as throat singing. Two women sing a **duet** back and forth. The singers make deep sounds in their throats that might remind you of ocean waves. The performers keep singing until one runs out of breath or laughs. Some Inuit artists, such as Tanya Tagaq (1975–), create modern songs with throat singing. You can listen to two young women perform throat singing in this video. How does the laughing affect the tone of the song?

🔍 *Globe Mail* Inuit throat singing

THE SCIENCE OF SOUND

WORDS TO KNOW

flat note: a note that is half a step lower than the natural note.

sharp note: a note that is half a step higher than the natural note.

As you might have noticed from watching the imaginary concert at the beginning of the chapter, some people have beautiful singing voices and other people do not. Of course, people have different ideas on what is beautiful music and what isn't, but in general there are some singers who most people agree are very accomplished—Aretha Franklin, Beyonce, and Freddie Mercury are all considered very talented singers. What made them great?

There are lots of answers to that question! A person who can sing with emotion and make their listeners feel something, too, might be considered a great singer. Someone who knows their music very well and hits all the right words with the right timing—that skill, too, lends itself to greatness. Getting the right pitch is very important as well! If you sing the wrong notes, you probably won't be considered a very good singer.

> Some singers or people who use their voices regularly for work, such as actors or teachers, can suffer vocal cord strain. This is when the muscles and vocal cords in the voice box are injured because of overuse.

Play some music on this website—no instrument needed! Try playing the same notes on two different instruments. How are the sounds similar? How are they different? Try playing a song on the virtual guitar. Can you make it sound pleasant to your ears? How about combining two different virtual instruments for a song? How do you get them to sound good together?

🔍 virtual instruments

Another element that makes a great singer has nothing to do with the science of sound—it's confidence. Some people love singing and know they can do it well and are comfortable singing in front of people. Those people are often considered great singers.

But an important thing to remember is that great singing requires practice. Nobody starts out as a great singer, just as nobody is great at doing a backflip the first time they try. Your larynx and voice box are made of muscles, and those muscles need training in order to become great. So, keep singing!

PITCH PERFECT

INSTRUMENTS

Thump, plink, and plunk! We have so many types of music we can listen to. How about the bouncy beats of pop or the driving rap of hip-hop? The delicate tinkle and sudden booms of classical piano? All are examples of music, no matter what type you prefer.

Musicians arrange notes with different pitches into patterns to create music. In Western music, there are 12 pitches. Seven of these are named with letters—A, B, C, D, E, F, and G—and are called natural notes. In between these notes are five other notes that are half steps up or down from the natural note. These are called flats and sharps. You might play an A flat or a C sharp. A **flat note** has a lower pitch and a **sharp note** has a higher pitch.

Before an orchestra plays, musicians tune their instruments so, when played, the sound waves blend.

Musicians arrange musical notes on staff paper that has four lines and five spaces. The higher the note is on the staff, the higher the sound. Lower notes on the staff represent lower sounds.

THE SCIENCE OF SOUND

> **WORDS TO KNOW**
>
> **varnish:** a liquid applied to a surface that dries to form a hard, transparent coating.
>
> **pollinator:** an insect or other animal that transfers pollen from the male part of a flower to the female part of a flower.
>
> **species:** a group of organisms that share common traits and can reproduce offspring.

All instruments rely on vibrations to make music. But a piano doesn't sound the same as a cello—even though they both use strings! With a piano, the player is tapping a hammer onto a string to make it vibrate, while a cellist moves a bow across the cello string to create vibration. These vibrations make different patterns of sound waves that sound different to our ears.

What about a cello and a violin? Both of those instruments use bows to vibrate their strings, so they must sound the same, right? No. Cellos and violins might seem similar, but they are different in size, shape, type of wood, thickness of materials—even the type of **varnish** affects the sound each instrument makes.

Just as stringed instruments sound very different from each other, wind instruments do, too. They create noise when the player uses their mouth to make a buzzing sound in the mouthpiece, which creates a standing wave in a wind instrument's tube.

Sweet Sound of Nectar

It might seem that only organisms with ears can hear sound, which would rule out plants, right? Hold on! Studies have shown that some plants can actually hear **pollinators** such as bees when they come close. How do we know this? Because when plants hear pollinators approach, they react by sweetening the nectar in hopes the pollinator will be more likely to catch a snack and do some pollinating in the process, helping ensure the survival of the plant **species**.

Scientists experimented with the evening primrose plant, exposing it to silence, the buzz of a bee about 4 inches away, and different sounds a computer makes. They measured the amount of nectar plants produced right after each sound. The plants that were exposed to buzzing bees made their nectar sweeter! It turns out, you don't need ears to sense vibrations and "hear" the world around you.

PITCH PERFECT

Brass instruments are a group of wind instruments, such as a French horn, trombone, trumpet, or tuba, with long metal tubes curved two or more times and ending in a flared bell. These instruments have valves or a slide that can be used to produce all the tones within the instrument's range. Trumpets have valves that change the length of the column and, therefore, the pitch. Trombone players change the length of the tube with a slide.

> **Listen to this piano scale.** Can you tell which notes are flats or sharps and which notes are natural? How do they sound different?
> 🔍 Pulse Berklee major scales

Trumpets and trombones make similar but different sounds because of their size, shape, and valves versus slide.

Trombones produce the lowest notes when the slide is all the way out, or fully extended.

Woodwind instruments are another group of wind instruments that also require air from the performer. A woodwind, such as a clarinet, flute, oboe, or saxophone, is a tube of wood or metal usually ending in a slightly flared bell. They produce tones by the vibration of one or two reeds in the mouthpiece or by the passing of air over a mouth hole and have finger holes or keys used to produce all the tones within an instrument's range. With flutes, players blow air into an opening, and with reed instruments, such as the saxophone, that air travels over a very thin piece of wood called a reed, which vibrates and creates the sound wave.

Now that we have looked at how people make and use sound, let's look at how humans recognize loud or soft sounds and how scientists measure the energy in sound. We'll find out why some sounds are loud and others are soft in the next chapter.

> **ESSENTIAL QUESTION**
>
> How do different creatures make different sounds?

TEXT TO WORLD

Do you play an instrument? What instrument family does it belong to? How does it produce sound?

BUILD A WIND INSTRUMENT

Musicians make sound with wind instruments by blowing air into them. You can make your own wind instrument and do some experiments to make different types of sound.

> **TOOL KIT**
> - science notebook and pencil
> - wax paper
> - cardboard toilet paper tube
> - rubber band
> - something pointy

▸ **Cut the wax paper so it's somewhat larger than the end of the toilet paper tube.**

▸ **Wrap the wax paper over the end of the tube and secure it with a rubber band.**

▸ **Have an adult help you to use a pencil or other pointy object to poke a hole in the wax paper.**

▸ **Ready to make music?** Place your finger over the hole and blow into the open end of the toilet paper tube. Don't blow as though you're blowing out birthday candles. Instead, hum or make your lips buzz (as though you were playing a kazoo) or even talk.

▸ **Experiment with opening and closing the hole in the tube.** Does the sound change when the hole is open? What happens if you add more holes?

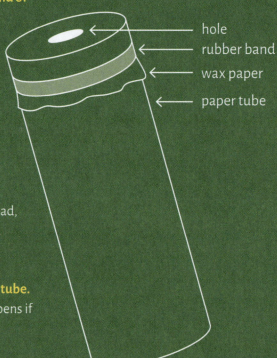

Try This!

Change the way you blow into the tube. Make your humming louder or softer. How does that affect the noise coming from your instrument?

MUSICAL GLASS

TOOL KIT
- science notebook and pencil
- 6 same-size jars
- a jug of water
- wooden spoon

Remember, sound waves travel differently through solids, liquids, and gases. Let's explore how sound vibrations travel through water. In this activity, you will make a xylophone with glass jars and water.

▸ **Start a scientific method worksheet in your science notebook.** What is your hypothesis? How will the pitch change with the water level? Organize your experiment in a chart.

▸ **Place the jars on a flat surface such as a table.** Fill the first jar almost full. Pour a little less water into the next jar, a little less in the next one, and so on, until all six jars have water.

▸ **Tap one jar at a time with the wooden spoon.** Record your observations.

▸ **Compare your results.** Which jar has the highest pitch? Which jar has the lowest pitch?

Method	Prediction	Result
Fullest jar		
Least full jar		

WHAT'S HAPPENING?

You make sound vibrations each time you hit a jar. The jar with the least amount of water vibrates the fastest, so it has the highest pitch. The jar with the most water vibrates the slowest. It has the lowest pitch.

Try This!

Arrange the jars from the lowest pitch to the highest pitch. Can you play a simple song on your water xylophone? Explore how to turn the jars into a musical scale by pouring out some of the water.

SOUND MAKER

Experiment with musical sounds. Let's see how two sound makers create different sounds.

▶ **In your science notebook, sketch two different sound makers that you can play in two different ways.** Include a note about what materials from the supplies list you are going to use and how you are going to build the sound makers.

▶ **Build and test your sound makers.** How many types of sounds can you make with each one? How loud can you make the sounds? How soft can you make the sounds?

Try This!

What regular instrument is your sound maker similar to? Try making a sound maker with two different notes.

TOOL KIT

- science notebook and pencil
- containers (yogurt tubs, ice cream containers, tin cans, boxes, etc.)
- fabric
- rubber bands
- plastic wrap, wax paper
- beans, rocks, or beads
- 2 paper tubes
- 2 paper plates
- construction paper
- scissors
- glue
- cotton balls
- tape
- pencils
- string

Ben's Singing Bowls

Ben Franklin (1706–1790) was an American statesman, musician, and inventor. Because of his love of music, Franklin created an instrument called the glass armonica. He attached 37 glass bowls to a spinning glass rod. Then, he rubbed a wet fingertip along the rims. The bowls sounded *spooky!* So spooky that people began to spread rumors that the high-pitched music caused hallucinations and madness. Some people wondered if lead-based paint used on the glass bowls made the players sick with lead poisoning. No scientific evidence was ever found against the innocent armonica.

Learn more about Franklin's invention and listen to an armonica in this video. How does the water affect the sound?

🔎 Ben Franklin armonica Toronto

58

BUILD A DRUM

Let's explore making sounds with a drum built from tin cans. The edges of the cans may be sharp, so have an adult assist you.

> **TOOL KIT**
> - scientific notebook and pencil
> - dish towel
> - can opener
> - tin cans (at least 3 cans of the same size)
> - duct tape or masking tape
> - wooden spoon
> - pencil

▶ **Start a scientific method worksheet in your science notebook.** What is your hypothesis? How will the length of the drum affect its sound? Which types of tin can drum will have the highest and the lowest sounds? Organize the experiment in a chart.

▶ Place the dish towel on a flat surface.

▶ Ask an adult to remove the bottoms from all the cans except for one.

▶ Place the can with the bottom on the dish towel.

▶ Stack a second can on top of the first and secure it with tape to create a short drum.

▶ **Place the drum open end up on the towel and strike it up and down with the spoon.** Can you make different sounds? Record your observations.

▶ **What will happen when you tape a third can on top?** Write down a prediction and repeat the last step.

▶ **Compare the results.** Which drum made the highest sound? Which drum made the lowest sound?

Wang Xiaolong of China is the Guinness World Record holder for the highest note sung by a male. He hit 5,243 Hz in 2017. Listen to him in this video. Can you even hear his highest notes?

🔍 Wang Xialong video

WHAT'S HAPPENING?

The air vibrates, making sound waves inside the drum. A long drum makes a low frequency sound louder, and a short one does the opposite.

Try This!

What would happen if you placed a hand over the opening of the drum? Why? Try it.

WARBLING WINEGLASSES

TOOL KIT
- science journal and pencil
- stemmed wineglasses of different sizes
- water
- metal spoon
- online keyboard

Where did Ben Franklin find the inspiration for the glass armonica? At a musical performance in London, the performer's instruments were wineglasses of different sizes filled with water. With a wet fingertip, the musician circled the rims of the glasses. The glasses responded to the friction in a variety of pitches, and the resulting vibrations produced ethereal, haunting sounds. Work with your classmates, friends, or family members to create warbling wineglasses. Experiment with varying water levels to create different pitches.

❯ **Start a scientific method worksheet to organize your questions and predictions.** How will the amount of water in each glass impact pitch? How much friction will be required to produce vibrations and sounds?

❯ **Experiment by pouring different amounts of water into the different wineglasses to create a full scale of notes.** You can use an online keyboard to establish the appropriate pitch for each note. Gently tap each glass with the spoon to test for a matching pitch.

* Is it easy to determine if the sounds are the same?
* How carefully do you need to listen?
* Does it help to have several people listen at the same time?
* How can you adjust the pitch in each glass so it matches the scale?

❯ **Practice playing tunes on the glasses.** Start with something simple, such as "Happy Birthday." Don't get frustrated if it doesn't work right away! Make sure your finger is wet enough. Then, mix it up! Play more complicated but familiar pieces. See if others can identify them.

Watch a wineglass performance by Robert Tiso. What do you notice about the wineglasses? About the water? How does this affect the sound he's able to produce?

🔎 Robert Tiso video

Ben Franklin's glass armonica
Credit: Tonamel (CC BY 2.0)

▶ **Work together to write a fantastical poem or story, and compose a musical piece that reflects the literary work's mood.** Ben Franklin penned a dramatic literary work to be performed with an accompanist on the glass armonica. Perform the work as someone accompanies you on the warbling wineglasses.

Try This!

Search for an online performance of a street musician playing wineglasses. You might be lucky enough to watch one in person! What do you notice about their playing technique? Explore glass armonica pieces by musician William Zeitler (1954–) with a family member or friend. What emotional responses do they ignite? Listen to Mozart's "Adagio and Rondo." These are delicate pieces he composed for the glass armonica. How do the pieces suit the instrument?

Chapter 4

ALL THAT
SOUND

Do you ever play your music *LOUDLY*? The volume creeps higher until the music travels all over the house. When other people are at home, you probably turn it down. The same music plays, but now it's more quiet.

ESSENTIAL QUESTION

What makes a sound louder or quieter?

Sounds such as the bark of a dog can be loud, while the meow of a kitten can be soft. Have you ever wondered what makes a sound loud or soft?

When you hear sounds, you are hearing energy—sound energy. Each sound wave carries a different amount of energy. Loud sounds have more energy than soft sounds.

ALL THAT SOUND

A traditional drum from Japan, called a taiko, has a powerful sound. When performers strike the taiko it vibrates, producing a rumbling sound. *BOOM, boom, BOOM*! The molecules in this sound wave carry a large amount of energy.

Look at the taiko players in this video. How does the size of the drum relate to the volume of the sound? How would you describe the sound of these drums?

🔍 taiko drum Ovation

Sometimes, to be heard better, people use megaphones to make themselves louder.

Sound waves with less energy are usually quieter to the human ear. What do you do when you don't want anyone to hear a secret? You whisper. *Shhhh!* A whisper sounds gentle to our ears because it has less energy than the sound from a drum.

Amplitude measures how much energy is in a sound wave. The loudness or softness of a sound wave depends on its amplitude. A sound wave with a larger amplitude produces a louder sound. A clap of thunder, the roar of a jet, and the whizz pop bang from fireworks are sound waves with higher amplitudes.

THE SCIENCE OF SOUND

WORDS TO KNOW

decibel (dB): a unit used to measure the loudness of a sound.

A sound wave with a smaller amplitude produces a softer sound. A whisper and our breath are sound waves with lower amplitudes.

And the amplitude of sound waves can change—turn up your television and the sound waves carrying that energy are increasing in energy. More energy means more sound.

Scientists measure amplitude in **decibels (dB)**. The number of decibels indicates how much energy a sound wave carries. The softest sound a human ear can hear is 0 dB. That would be similar to a leaf falling on the grass. Where would your breath be on the decibel scale? Try listening to it and take a guess. A breath is about 10 dB. And the sound wave from rustling leaves carries the same amount of energy.

Have you ever covered your ears when a gas-powered lawnmower starts up? The sound of its engine measures 90 dB. A rock concert has an even louder amplitude. It typically registers at 120 dB. And the blast of a rocket produces about 190 dB in sound energy!

Which amplitude produces the louder sound?

The decibel was named for Alexander Graham Bell (1847–1922), the inventor of the telephone.

Your hearing can be damaged if you keep listening to sounds higher than 85 dB. That's why people wear ear protection at loud concerts and when operating loud machinery.

ALL THAT SOUND

PROTECT THE EARS!

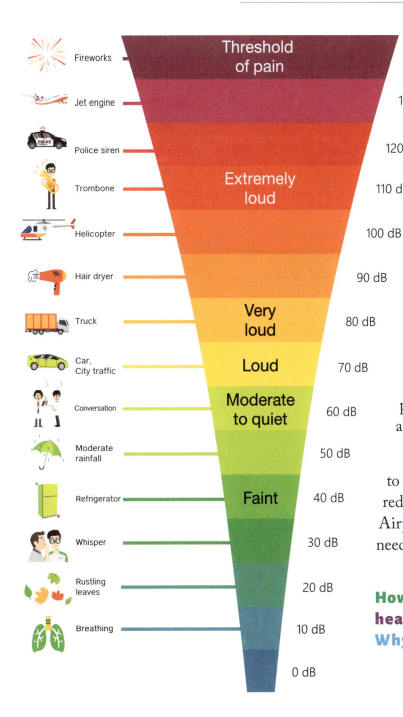

Some professions require workers to be in very loud environments. Airplane pilots, for example, have to deal with many sources of noise in the cockpit, including the roar of engines and the whir of propellers. They need a way to block these loud noises out to save their ears, but they also need to be able to communicate with their co-pilots, air traffic controllers, and others.

Headsets allow pilots to talk to each other while reducing harmful noise. Airport workers on the ground need that ear protection, too.

How can you protect your hearing from loud sounds? Why is it important to do so?

THE SCIENCE OF SOUND

WORDS TO KNOW

patent: a right given to only one inventor to manufacture, use, or sell an invention for a certain number of years.

supersonic: faster than the speed of sound.

speed of sound: the speed at which sound travels. In the air at sea level, this is 755 miles per hour.

pressure waves: waves that create variations of pressure in whatever material they are passing through.

shock wave: a sharp change of pressure moving through the air, caused by something moving faster than the speed of sound.

sonic boom: the sound created by an object traveling through the air faster than the speed of sound.

Ambulance drivers, construction workers, factory workers, landscapers, and people who work at concert venues need ear protection. It enables all of these people to do their jobs and maintain their hearing.

Ear plugs were **patented** in 1884, but the technology has changed since then. Instead of passive ear protection, which simply acts as a barrier between the noise and the ear, active ear protection uses technology to suppress loud noise while allowing softer noises, such as voices, to be heard. Loud noise above 82 dB is suppressed, while noise that is below 82 dB can pass.

In the city of Delft in the Netherlands, most of the roads are paved with porous asphalt—that means there are tiny empty spaces in the roadway that absorb sound, making the city quieter than other cities.

SOAR!

On October 14, 1947, test pilot Chuck Yeager (1923–2020) climbed into the cockpit of an experimental aircraft. The Bell X-1 was the first **supersonic** test aircraft. In the 1940s, no aircraft engine was powerful enough to propel the plane, so it used a rocket engine. A bomber carried the X-1 into flight to conserve fuel. Once in the air, Chuck let the X-1 accelerate. That day, he became the first person to fly faster than the **speed of sound**!

> You can watch Chuck Yeager break the sound barrier in this news segment from 1947. Do you notice anything different from this clip compared to televised news of today?
>
> 🔍 King Rose Chuck Yeager

66

ALL THAT SOUND

Chuck Yeager

Now, jet aircraft are even faster. Some planes set world records. One of the fastest jets in the world is the X-43. It can fly up to 7,000 miles per hour. This is nearly 10 times the speed of sound!

When a jet travels through the sky, it pushes air molecules away, creating **pressure waves**. As the jet approaches the speed of sound, the sound waves cannot get out of the way fast enough. They pile up in a **shock wave**. When the jet flies faster than the speed of sound, energy releases from the shock wave with a boom. This sound is called a **sonic boom**. At 110 dB, it's one of the loudest sounds in the world.

LOCAL NOISE POLLUTION

Wave troughs are the opposite of peaks—they are the lowest point of the wave.

A leaf blower buzzes outside the window. A loudspeaker blasts a recorded message. Overhead, a low-flying aircraft zooms out of view. What do these sounds have in common? They can be annoying and unpleasant. Most people don't want to listen to these noises, at least not for extended lengths of time.

THE SCIENCE OF SOUND

WORDS TO KNOW

noise pollution: unwanted or harmful sounds on the land, in the air, or in water.

repel: a force that pushes things away.

Scientists call unwanted sounds **noise pollution**. When noise pollution is constant, it can harm our health and affect our hearing.

Researchers have confirmed that noise causes stress. It keeps some people awake at night and can lead to hearing loss and high blood pressure. In one study, after working in a noisy factory for only half a day, workers had significant rises in their heart rates and blood pressure measurements. One small study even showed that exposure to traffic noise had an effect on cancer outcomes. Sleep is a very important part of healthy living, and if a person's sleep is interrupted because of noise, that can increase their chances of getting sick.

Scientists have also studied the effects of noise on children. Sources of noise pollution include loud toys and tablets, computers, and music players—plus there is environmental noise pollution that varies depending on where they live. All of this has an impact on kids. One study showed students did worse on tests when decibel levels rose.

> **Do you think you live somewhere noisy?** Does your classroom always seem loud? You can test it yourself! With permission from an adult, use a smartphone app to measure sounds where you live. What do you find? How can you protect your ears from loud places?
>
> 🔍 sound meter

Booming

NASA is designing a very quiet, very fast aircraft. In January 2024, NASA and Lockheed Martin unveiled their supersonic airplane that can travel without creating a loud sonic boom. How? The front of the plane has a thin, tapered nose that makes up a third of the plane's length. That shape spreads out the supersonic shockwaves that typically create loud sonic booms that can be heard from the ground. The nose is so skinny, the cockpit has to settle about halfway down the length of the plane—and the pilot doesn't get a forward-facing window! Instead, the plane uses a series of cameras that feed real-time images to a monitor that the pilot uses to navigate.

ALL THAT SOUND

What about organisms other than humans? What happens when animals and insects and even plants are exposed to lots of noise? Scientists have discovered that noise pollution can interrupt communication between animals that use sound to attract mates, warn others of danger, or try to find their offspring or packs in a crowd. Predator animals such as owls and cats, which rely on finely tuned hearing to catch their prey, have lower success rates in areas with more noise.

How did the howler monkey earn its name?
Its incredible roar can reach 140 dB.
That's as loud as the deck of an aircraft carrier!

Even plants can be affected by sound pollution! Plants rely on pollinators to spread their seeds and reproduce. Some pollinators are attracted to certain noises, and some are **repelled** by noise. What happens if a plant is growing in an environment with lots of repellent noise? It might not host enough pollinators to reproduce. Noise pollution can upset the balance of species in an environment.

Listen to some classroom sounds here. Which classroom sound annoys you the most? What are some ways you could lower the sound volume in your classroom?

🔎 thinglink classroom sounds

What can we do about noise pollution? Lots! For individuals, wearing ear protection around loud noises is an easy way to stay healthy. Many people even wear headphones to concerts! Any time someone works in a factory or operates a chainsaw or other loud equipment, they should wear ear protection.

Noise-cancelling headphones are a great way to keep loud noises from damaging your ears!

THE SCIENCE OF SOUND

The U.S government passed the Noise Control Act in 1972. This act helped cut noise levels from cars, planes, machinery, appliances, and other items that could harm our health. The Noise Control Act wasn't funded after 1982, so the responsibility for noise levels shifted to state and local governments.

At home and at school, things such as rugs, plants, fabric panels, and curtains can all help a space be quieter. Have you ever seen chairs at school with tennis balls on the feet? That's another way to reduce noise pollution! The tennis balls muffle the noise made when chairs are moved around.

> **Watch this NASA video on the different parts of a sound wave.** Why are some sounds louder and some sounds quieter?
>
> 🔍 NASA parts sound wave

On a larger scale, during the 1970s, engineers devised large walls to act as noise barriers to be built around highways and airports and other places where lots of noise is created. These walls are often made from concrete, wood, plastic, aluminum—sometimes even dirt! Noise barriers work to reduce both noise and air pollution, but there are some drawbacks.

ALL THAT SOUND

They can get in the way of people's views, for one thing. And in some places, graffiti artists can't help but be drawn to the blank canvas a noise barrier presents.

If large walls aren't an option, planting trees, bushes, and other green spaces around high-traffic, loud areas works, too!

Another way people try to reduce noise pollution around the world is by designing and building quieter modes of transportation. Electric cars, for example, are not only quieter than gas cars, they're also better for the environment, as they don't release pollution. Engineers have also designed quieter trucks, buses, trains, and planes.

> **Austrian physicist Ernst Mach (1838-1916) figured out how to measure airspeed relative to the speed of sound.** When a plane is flying at the speed of sound, it is said to be going Mach 1. Mach 2 is twice the speed of sound, Mach 3 is three times the speed of sound, and so on. Watch a film about a sonic boom on this website. Have you ever heard a sonic boom? What might it be like to test aircraft for NASA?
>
>
>
> 🔍 NASA sonic boom video

Rumble

Black clouds roll in. You rush inside as lightning flashes through the sky. Suddenly, there's a deep rumble. *Clack! Clack! Boom!*

Have you ever wondered why you see lightning before you hear the thunder? Light waves travel faster than sound waves. The speed of light is 186,282 miles per second. If you could travel at the speed of light, you could loop Earth not once, not twice, but seven and a half times in only one second!

Sound takes sound approximately 5 seconds to travel 1 mile. Next time you see the flash of lightning, count the number of seconds until you hear the thunder. Take this number and divide it by five. You will then know how many miles away the storm is.

THE SCIENCE OF SOUND

WORDS TO KNOW

evolution: the process of living things gradually changing to adapt to the world around them.

dopamine: a chemical in the brain that improves your mood and lowers stress.

SOOTHING SOUNDS

Now that we've talked about harmful noises, let's turn our attention to pleasant noises! Ah, that's better.

Many people find the sounds of nature to be soothing and relaxing. Close your eyes and think about what a busy city street sounds like. Now, imagine taking a walk in a forest and noticing what sounds you hear there. How are the sounds different? How does each environment make you feel?

The sound waves we hear from birds chirping and bees humming are generally pleasant to the ear. The sounds might make us think of a rainforest. The sound of waves on a beach, of a breeze in the leaves, of a stream full of running water—all of these make for a pleasant, soothing listening experience.

> **Noise pollution affects creatures other than people!** Look at this video to learn more. How can we protect the natural world from noise pollution?
>
> 🔍 SciShow noise pollution
>
>

Why? Why do some sounds make many of us feel good? Some researchers point toward **evolution** to help explain our relationship with sound. Modern cities haven't been around for very long. Humans use to spend their days in the natural world, surrounded by the sounds we now try to recreate on phone apps to help us sleep. It makes sense that our brains react to natural sounds with happier moods and lower heart rates.

What kinds of sounds do you think you'll hear on this forest pathway?

ALL THAT SOUND

Forest 404

Scientists in the United Kingdom used pleasant sounds in an experiment called Forest 404 to see if listening to sounds in nature made people feel better. More than 7,000 people in the United Kingdom took part in the 2019 study. Researchers from Forest 404 are still sorting through their data and finding conclusions. However, experiments conducted by other scientists have already shown that soothing sounds calm the human body. Also, they help some people to concentrate and sleep better.

Listen to some nature sounds at this website. How do the sounds make you feel?

🔎 BBC nature sounds

Dopamine is a hormone in the human brain that helps messages travel between nerve cells. When you do something that feels good—such eat a bowl of your favorite ice cream or spend time with a friend—your brain produces lots of dopamine. Scientists have found that hearing pleasant sounds does the same thing—causes your brain to release dopamine. This feel-good chemical affects many functions in your body, including memory, motivation, mood, heart rate, and learning.

Some people listen to pleasant sounds as they fall asleep. The noise helps them relax and allows their minds to let go of the day's events.

ESSENTIAL QUESTION

What makes a sound louder or quieter?

For humans, sound can be a good experience or a bad experience. On a deeper level, sound is a very useful tool! We can use sound waves for lots of different things—even exploration. Let's take a look in the next chapter.

TEXT TO **WORLD**

Do certain sounds make you feel better or worse? Why?

SOUND STORY

TOOL KIT
- science notebook and pencil
- recording device

Sounds tell us so much about our world. Honking cars mean there's traffic on a busy street. A pulsing bell tells us a crosswalk is ahead. Create a story using only sounds.

> **Begin by writing down a story title and approximately five story points in your notebook.** Look at the example below.

The Missing Homework
- My alarm wakes me up. (Record alarm sound.)
- I get dressed. (Record the sound of dresser drawers and closet hangers.)
- My homework is missing! (Record sound of riffling papers on a desk.)
- Could it be the dog? (Record your dog.)
- Could I have thrown it out? (Record the garbage can lid opening and closing.)
- Mystery solved! (Record sound of opening backpack—homework is there!)

> **Using a recording device, collect sounds for the story or use the sound makers you created in Chapter 3 to make sound effects.**

> **Play the sounds for yourself.** Do the sounds capture the points from your story?

> **Read the title of the story to a friend and then play the sounds.** Ask the friend to describe what they think is happening.

A nightingale floor is a type of wooden floor built by Japanese engineers approximately 400 years ago. They designed the floor to squeak when stepped on. The squeak alerted guards to possible thieves or spies.

Try This!

How could you layer and repeat the sounds? What are some other sounds you could add to your story?

TUNE BOOSTER

IDEAS FOR SUPPLIES
- internet access
- science journal
- posterboard
- markers or colored pencils

A loudspeaker makes sounds louder. Inside the speaker is a cone that amplifies sound vibrations. Let's see how this works with everyday objects.

> **Start a scientific method worksheet in your science notebook.** What is your hypothesis? How will the glass bowl, paper cone, and toilet roll boost the sound of the smartphone? Which object will boost sound the most? Organize your experiment in a chart.

> **Place the smartphone on a smooth table.** Find a song and play it. Stand a few feet away from the phone. Can you hear the song? Record your observations.

> **Repeat the experiment, but this time put the smartphone in the glass bowl.** Does the sound change? If so, how? Record your observations.

> **Fold the paper into a cone and tape it to the smartphone's speaker.** Repeat step 2.

> **Use the scissors to make a slit in the toilet roll.** Put the phone, speaker side down, into the slit. Repeat step 2.

> **Compare your results.** Which object amplified the sound the most? How do you know? How might you make a sound booster out of two different types of materials?

Shhhhhh . . .

An onion-like room nestled in the headquarters of Microsoft in Redmond, Washington, is the quietest place built by humans. The company spent two years building this special room to test the sound vibrations of its equipment. In 2015, the room set the world record for silence at minus 20.6 dB! How quiet is this? Engineers who work in the room can hear their blood rushing around their body and their eyeballs squelching! Would you want to be in a room like that?

Try This!

Repeat your experiment using other ways to amplify your music. What works best?

MUSIC
WHILE YOU WORK

> **TOOL KIT**
> - science notebook and pencil
> - this book
> - computer
> - headphones

Some people enjoy listening to music when they are studying. In this activity, let's see if your music helps you to concentrate.

> **Start a scientific method worksheet in your science notebook.** What is your hypothesis? How will music affect your concentration? Will you be able to remember more with no music, music at a low volume, or music through headphones? Which will be the most distracting? Organize your experiment in a chart.

> **Open this book to a page you haven't read before and read it with no music on.** How easy is it to concentrate? Can you remember the first sentence without looking? Was there an image on the page? Record your observations in your science notebook.

> **Play your music at a low volume and read a new page in this book.** Answer the questions in step 2.

> **Put on your headphones and repeat step 2.** Compare your results. What do you notice?

The human ear can hear sounds as low as 20 Hz and as high as 20,000 Hz, although not everyone can hear sounds as low and high as these. The ear is most sensitive to sounds made by vibrations between 1,000 and 5,000 Hz.

Try This!

Read a page from this book with the music turned up. Did the results change? How can you use this information to study more effectively?

MUFFLING
SOUND

Sounds can be more than loud. They can boom and blast and blare. We can solve the problem of unwanted sounds by using materials that muffle or absorb these noises. Let's see how well everyday objects absorb sound waves.

> **TOOL KIT**
> - science notebook and pencil
> - smartphone or timer
> - newspaper
> - bubble wrap
> - fabric
> - cardboard box
> - winter coat

▶ **In your science notebook, predict which material will block the most and the least sound.**

▶ **Set an alarm to ring on the smartphone.**

▶ **Take one material at a time from the list.** Wrap the ringing phone in the material. Write your observations in your science notebook.

▶ **Compare your results with your prediction.**

Try This!

Which material worked best at muffling the sound? Why do you think this was? Using what you know, turn a shoebox into a soundproof box by combining materials to muffle sound. With permission from an adult, use a sound meter app to test your results.

Career Connection

An audio engineer, also called a sound engineer, records, mixes, and produces sound. Music is recorded in tracks, and those tracks are layered together and adjusted so the sound quality is the best it can be—that's the job of an audio engineer. You can often find them in the mixing booth in recording studios, watching and listening as musicians play and sing, adjusting the sound until it's perfect. Some audio engineers work at live concert venues, making sure the show has the right sound quality. Movies and television shows use sound engineers, too, to produce sounds and dialogue that are authentic to the scenes. There are schools that offer degrees in audio engineering, and you might even find camps and classes for kids and teens—it's never too early to take a class and start building your portfolio of work!

Chapter 5

SOUND
TECHNOLOGY

"Welcome aboard!" Imagine you are working on a research vessel. Your job is to investigate the seafloor. The ship has bunk beds, computers, and labs for specimens but no diving equipment. How will you explore the ocean floor without diving equipment? Don't worry, you won't need it. Instead of diving equipment, you are going to use sound to study the seafloor.

ESSENTIAL QUESTION

What else are sound waves used for?

Scientists use sound to deepen their understanding of how Earth works. For example, sound can help scientists explore underwater volcanoes, study **coral reefs**, or create maps of the ocean floor. Using sound, scientists can also learn more about **marine** animals and then use this information to better protect the animals. Let's learn more about sound and exploration.

SOUND TECHNOLOGY

SONAR

Sound is helpful to ocean scientists because sound waves travel farther in water than **radar** or light waves. Sonar equipment called a transmitter sends out sound waves into the water. When those sound waves hit something that isn't water, such as a rocky ledge or a marine animal or a coral reef, the waves bounce back toward the ship, where the equipment can detect the echo or reflected sound. The sonar equipment then measures the time it takes for the sound to travel to an object and bounce back.

Remember learning about echolocation in Chapter 2? Sonar uses the same principles. Sound waves are emitted from a source and researchers at that source study how the sound waves return after bumping against objects underwater.

On ships, sonar is used for navigation. On submarines, it alerts crews to other vessels. Scientists also use sonar to discover underwater **hazards**, map the ocean floor, and search for objects such as shipwrecks.

> **WORDS TO KNOW**
>
> **coral reef:** an underwater **ecosystem** that grows in warm ocean waters and is home to millions of creatures.
>
> **ecosystem:** a community of living and nonliving things and their environment. Living things are plants, animals, and insects. Nonliving things are soil, rocks, and water.
>
> **marine:** having to do with the ocean.
>
> **radar:** a system that detects objects by bouncing radio waves off them and measuring how long it takes for the waves to return.
>
> **hazard:** a danger or risk.

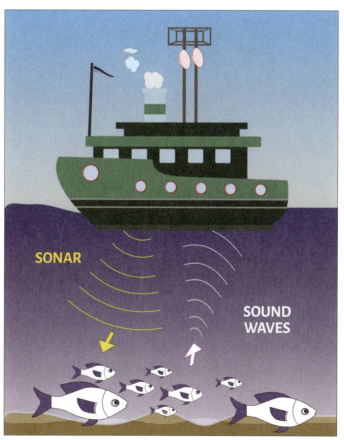

THE SCIENCE OF SOUND

WORDS TO KNOW

active sonar: a wave of energy sent out to measure how it's reflected back.

transducer: a device that changes one form of energy into another.

transponder: a device for receiving a radio signal and automatically transmitting a different signal.

passive sonar: a system that detects waves from a source.

hydrophone: a microphone that detects sound waves in the ocean.

plumb line: a length of rope used to find the depth in a body of water.

plumb bob: a small weight attached to a line and used as a level or to measure depth.

Sonar can be active or passive. **Active sonar** has a **transducer** that sends out high-frequency sound pulses called pings. When the pings reach an object, the transducer receives the echoes that come back from the object. The transducer can then calculate the distance to the object.

Active sonar can pick up signals from objects miles away and set a ship's course at sea. To do this, the transducer picks up sounds from beacons known as **transponders** anchored to the ocean floor. Each transponder has a unique sound signal. Computers on the ship receive the signals and can then set a course for the ship.

Passive sonar does not send out transmissions. It collects sound echoes with an underwater microphone called a **hydrophone**. The hydrophone listens and picks up sound energy. It then changes the sound energy into electrical energy. Some scientists use computer programs to help them filter and identify these sounds.

Bat Signals

Echolocation is like sonar. Bats are an example of animals that use echolocation to find their way at night and locate food. Bats make high-pitched sounds. These sound waves bounce off objects. Bats can then judge the distance to an object based on the echo. Try this activity with a partner to see how echolocation works. Put on a blindfold. Find your partner by listening to claps. To begin, clap your hands once. The partner claps back twice to mimic an echo. Your partner should not move. Keep clapping and listening to the "echo" until you have found your partner. What happens? Which of the five senses did you use?

SOUND TECHNOLOGY

SONAR AND THE OCEAN FLOOR

In centuries past, people didn't know what was hiding under the sea. Could there be mermaids or squid-like monsters, some wondered? How deep was the water? Until the 1900s, the only way to know the depth of the ocean was for sailors to dangle a long rope, called a **plumb line**, over the side of a ship. The rope had a weight called a **plumb bob** attached to its end. When the plumb bob hit the sea bottom, the sailor read the measurements marked along the rope's length to figure out the depth.

The *Challenger* Expedition between 1872 and 1876 was the first expedition organized to gather data about the ocean. The HMS *Challenger* departed from England in 1872 and traveled 68,890 miles, through the South Atlantic, around the southern tip of Africa, across the Indian Ocean and the Antarctic Circle, to Australia, New Zealand, the Hawaiian Islands, back south to the southern tip of South American where the Pacific and Atlantic Oceans meet. Finally, it went back to England with a vessel full of data and samples.

Hydrophones can listen to signals as far as 3,000 miles away.

Painting of the HMS *Challenger* by William Frederick Mitchell

THE SCIENCE OF SOUND

WORDS TO KNOW

archaeologist: a scientist who studies people through the objects they left behind.

The crew included six scientists who oversaw the scientific aspects of the journey. They discovered 4,700 new species of plants and animals! And they made nearly 500 depth soundings. This was when they dropped a plumb line attached to a rope as deep as it would go and measured the distance. Their deepest sounding was 26,850 feet—more than 4 miles deep! Later, this area became known as Challenger Deep. It's part of the Mariana Trench and it is still the deepest known point of the earth's seabed.

Ancient Greek scientist Aristotle was was one of the first people to study sound. He conducted experiments into why people can hear underwater. He also suggested sound travels in waves.

Leonardo da Vinci had already remarked on the way sound waves could travel through water in 1490, and Swiss physicist Daniel Colladon (1802–1893) was able to measure the speed of sound waves in 1826. In 1906, American naval architect Lewis Nixon (1861–1940) introduced a device that used sound waves to detect icebergs and laid the foundation for more sonar inventions.

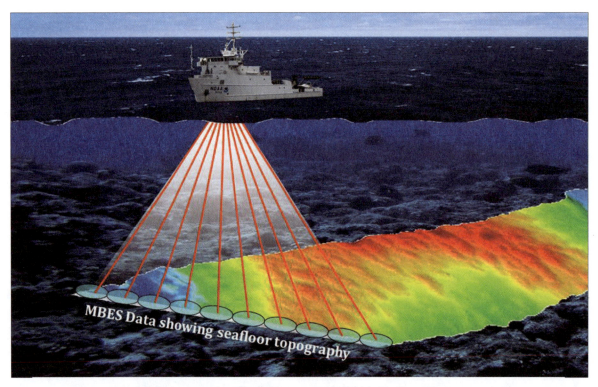

Artist's conception of multibeam sonar on NOAA ship *Nancy Foster*
Credit: NOS/NCCOS/CCMA (CC BY 2.0)

SOUND TECHNOLOGY

In 1912, the *Titanic* hit an iceberg and sank, killing more than 1,500 passengers on a ship that was marketed as "unsinkable." This tragedy spurred research into sonar techniques to detect obstacles in the water. When World War I broke out, researchers worked hard to improve ways of detecting enemy submarines underwater.

Watch this video to learn more about sound and the ocean. Why is it useful to be able to see the floor of an ocean, river, or lake? How can that help people?

🔍 sound scapes usoceangov

These early inventions all used passive sonar—no initiating sounds were sent out. But soon after the war, both England and the United States were building systems that included a sound wave projector and a receiver, making these active sonar systems.

Ocean acoustics is a branch of science that deals with sound in the sea.

The word "sonar" was first used in the United States during World War II, and the technology has continued to improve. Now, multibeam sonar systems can map an area much more quickly. And sonar isn't restricted to above-water ships! Autonomous underwater vehicles (AUVs) can make journeys deep into the ocean and use sonar in places that are very difficult for people to travel to.

Treasure

In 1708, English warships sank a Spanish ship off the coast of Colombia. The ship was carrying approximately 600 people, all of whom died, as well as precious treasures from Peru destined for Spain. The ship and its cargo remained at the bottom of the Caribbean Sea until 2015, when marine **archaeologists** discovered the ship using sonar. Dives to the wreck revealed cannons carved with dolphins and a billion dollars worth of gold, silver, and jewels.

THE SCIENCE OF SOUND

WORDS TO KNOW

pinger: a device that produces a pulsing sound wave.

It's because of sonar that scientists have salvaged wrecked ships, mapped regions of the ocean floor, and developed navigation and communication techniques with submarines and oceancraft. Fishermen use sonar to find large schools of fish. The oil industry uses sonar to discover geological formations where oil and gas might be found. After an oil spill, sonar can be used to find oil plumes, making cleanup a little more efficient. Some researchers use sonar to monitor the health and well-being of marine ecosystems, which is especially important as climate change becomes an increasingly crucial issue.

SOUND AND MARINE LIFE

Scientists use sound to protect marine animals. Nylon fishing nets are one danger that marine animals face. Each year, thousands of marine animals, including dolphins, accidentally get caught in these nets.

Seabed 2030

Although we have been using sonar for a long time, scientists have mapped less than 90 percent of the ocean floor! A detailed map of the entire seabed would help scientists develop climate models, track and predict weather patterns, organize cables and pipelines, and much more. In 2017, a new sonar project called Seabed 2030 began. For 13 years, scientists using sonar-equipped ships hope to map all the world's oceans. And the data they collect is going to be free for everyone all over the globe to use. Think of all the amazing discoveries to come!

Take a look at the work of Seabed 2030. Why is it important that the whole world has stakes in this project?

Seabed 2030

SOUND TECHNOLOGY

Scientists are turning to sound waves to reduce the risk to marine animals of becoming entangled in nets. One type of net uses a device called a **pinger** that puts out a low-frequency audible alarm. This sound alerts dolphins and porpoises and other animals of the presence of nets so animals can avoid them.

The speed of sound is influenced by temperature. Heat makes molecules move faster. When molecules vibrate faster, sound waves travel more swiftly

Many types of commercial fishing nets include pingers. But pingers are not perfect. Some parts of the net remain unprotected. Pingers also run on batteries, so fishing crews must constantly replace them. And some marine animals get used to the pinging sound and don't stay away.

Instead of using pingers, some fishing nets are coated in a chemical that stiffens the fibers. A stiffer net is better at reflecting sound waves. Animals that use echolocation may be able to better detect the nets and avoid becoming trapped in them.

Watch this video to learn more about mapping the ocean. Why is this work important?

🔍 Nat Geo see ocean floor

85

THE SCIENCE OF SOUND

WORDS TO KNOW

forage: to search for food.

breed: to produce offspring.

biology: the science of life and living things.

physics: the science of matter, energy, and forces in the universe and how they interact with each other. A scientist who studies physics is a physicist.

habitat: a plant's or animal's home, which supplies it with food, water, and shelter.

drought: a long period of little or no rain.

greenhouse gas: a gas in the atmosphere that traps the sun's heat.

atmosphere: the mixture of gases surrounding Earth.

Industrial Revolution: a period of time beginning in the late 1700s when people started using machines to make things in large factories.

fossil fuels: a source of energy that comes from plants and animals that lived millions of years ago. These include coal, oil, and natural gas.

Career Connection

An acoustician is someone who specializes in the study of sound. A marine bioacoustician is someone who studies how sound impacts marine organisms. These scientists observe how underwater noise helps or hurts creatures as they hunt, **forage**, **breed**, hide from predators, and travel in groups. The amount of sound in the lakes and oceans has been increasing since the Industrial Age began, as we send more and more ships across the sea and use large machinery to drill for oil and gas. Marine bioacousticians are part of the team that studies the impact and issues guidelines for noise control that help underwater environments stay healthy. **Biology**, computer science, **physics**, and math are all important parts of this field of study.

In addition to using sound to try to protect marine animals, scientists use sound in their research. For example, by studying the sounds in different coral reefs, scientists can put together a picture of different **habitats** and species in the reefs. Sound monitoring also lets scientists know about changes to the reefs. Healthier reefs have more sounds and a greater diversity of marine life.

Sound is even playing a part in restoring the health of coral reefs. Scientists discovered that setting up speakers in an unhealthy reef to play earlier recordings of that reef when it was healthy can actually make the reef healthier! The sounds of health attract young sea creatures that are in search of a suitable habitat. As more healthy creatures move in, the whole neighborhood improves.

SOUND TECHNOLOGY

Many types of fish have a swim bladder, a gas-filled organ that helps them control their buoyancy, or how they rise and sink in the water. This swim bladder also acts as a chamber that can produce and detect sound.

SOUND AND CLIMATE CHANGE

Have you noticed more news reports about severe storms? Earth's weather patterns are changing. We are seeing more and more evidence of a climate crisis in the form of an increased number of wildfires, more intense **drought**, bigger storms, and more frequent flooding. It may also mean periods of extreme heat, rising sea levels, and heavy rainfall.

Some climate change is natural, but recent climate change is much greater than what could occur naturally. **Greenhouse gases** such as carbon dioxide are one cause of climate change. These gases trap heat in the **atmosphere** and make the temperature on Earth rise. Since the **Industrial Revolution** began during the 1700s, our use of **fossil fuels** in manufacturing and transportation has caused a huge increase in those greenhouse gases, and our planet is getting hotter and hotter.

Arctic Sounds

In the past, much of the sound you might hear underwater in the Arctic Circle was natural, not manmade. But as the oceans have warmed as a result of climate change, the sounds are changing, too. Shipping routes have opened up and the noise of that traffic can affect wildlife and underwater habitats. Beluga whales hear the sounds of ice being broken up by ships and flee. Narwhals change how they vocalize and head toward shore when they're exposed to ship noise. Seals are also triggered to escape when confronted with noise. What can we do? Slower speeds mean less noise. Ships powered by renewable energy such as solar and wind are quieter than those that use fossil fuels. Mandatory noise regulations would go a long way in keeping the Arctic a safe place for wildlife. And education is always key! The more people know about noise pollution and how it affects wildlife, the more people will support measures to curb it.

THE SCIENCE OF SOUND

WORDS TO KNOW

dissonant: musical notes that do not sound good played together.

phonograph: a machine that picks up and reproduces the sounds recorded in the grooves cut into a record.

As the planet's temperature rises, so do ocean temperatures. Scientists use satellites to study the effect of climate change on the ocean. But satellites measure only changes at the ocean surface.

In the future, scientists could use sound to measure ocean temperatures. Because sound travels faster in warmer water, scientists could monitor increases in ocean temperature to understand the effects of climate change. For this to work, ships would have to lower hydrophones all over the ocean. Scientists would then need to collect and study the data.

Between 1890 and 1932, visitors to the Théâtrophone could pay a few coins and listen to an opera or theater performance over a telephone line. The Théâtrophone had two headphones and is one of the first immersive sound experiences—besides, of course, live performance.

Climate change means storms tend to be more intense and cause destructive flooding, such as the devastation wrought by Hurricane Harvey in Texas in 2017.
Credit: Jill Carlson (CC BY 2.0)

SOUND TECHNOLOGY

Boo!

Have you ever watched a scary movie? What made it scary? What kind of soundtrack did it use? Horror movies use music and other noise to make viewers afraid. A horror movie would land quite differently if the music was light and happy. Some of the techniques sound engineers use are music with minor chords, lowering the level of sound during an intense moment and then having a huge burst of sound for the jump scare, instruments that sound like screaming or creaking doors, and chords that don't sound nice together and are instead **dissonant**. Dissonance creates a feeling of uneasiness in the listener—perfect for horror movies!

Listen to the theme music for the 1978 horror film *Halloween*. What do you notice about it? How does it make you feel?

🔍 *Halloween* theme music

IMMERSIVE AUDIO

Modern technology has had a giant impact on the world of sound. From the invention of **phonographs** in 1877, which used needles bouncing on tinfoil to record the sounds and play them back, to today's systems that let you play music in a way that makes it feel live, technology has been an essential partner in improving the way we interact with sound.

Put on headphones and watch this commercial for speakers. What does it sound like? Does it feel as though the sounds are coming from different directions?

🔍 Genelec immersive audio reality

Have you ever been in a movie theater and felt as though the birds on the screen were chirping behind you? Or that a rocket ship was blasting off over to your right? Or that one of the characters was whispering in your left ear?

THE SCIENCE OF SOUND

> **WORDS TO KNOW**
>
> **immersive audio:** a three-dimensional sound experience that feels like listening to real life.
>
> **binocular vision:** to use two eyes to see.
>
> **binaural hearing:** hearing with two ears.
>
> **spatial audio:** a method of producing sound so it feels as though it's coming from more than one source.

Immersive audio is about experiencing sound from a movie, television show, or song in a way that feels like real life. When you're walking through your school, not all of the voices come from one speaker, right? These noises come from in front, behind, to the side, and even above. Engineers developed ways of replicating this experience for listeners in movie theaters, concert halls, and even at home.

Have you ever tried catching a ball with one eye closed? It's more difficult than catching it with both eyes open. **Binocular vision** lets your brain determine the position of the ball far better than when you're working with just one eye.

It's the same for ears. Most people have two, which makes it possible to figure out where a sound is coming from. If a dog barks right in front of you, that sound will reach both your ears at the same time. If the dog moves a few jumps to the left, when he barks again, your left ear will catch those sound waves sooner than your right ear. Your brain will be able to know that the sound is coming from the left.

SOUND TECHNOLOGY

How do we use **binaural hearing** to enjoy movies today? Speakers and software. Multiple speakers placed at different locations in a room—including at varying heights—makes it possible to release sounds from multiple sources. And sound engineers use software to direct which speakers different sounds will flow from.

> **Binaural hearing was very important when early humans had to be able to run from the predators they heard in the woods!**

How might immersive audio work with headphones? After all, there's no way to cart several speakers around on your head.

Engineers have come up with **spatial audio**, a way of producing sound that mimics biaural hearing. Music that's been processed with certain software can sound as though it's coming from different locations, even if it's all simply streaming into your headphones.

Sound—it's all around us. From the ring of the morning alarm tone to the chatter at the lunch table to the laugh track on your favorite show, sound is a huge part of our lives. Understanding the science behind how it travels and how we hear it is an essential part of better understanding our world and how we might take care of it.

And sound is part of human connection as well. The sound of your friends' laughter, your family's voices, and your favorite music—these are what make us who we are.

ESSENTIAL QUESTION

What else are sound waves used for?

We are learning more and more about sound and developing advanced technologies to manipulate it in ways that can help the planet and all who live on it. Maybe you'll be one of the researchers who comes up with a way to use sound waves to help protect different species or finds new ways of communicating. It's an exciting time to study sound!

TEXT TO WORLD

Have you ever listened to music with a record player? Does it sound different from music from a phone or radio?

SONAR
SOUND MAZE

TOOL KIT
- obstacles such as chairs or boxes
- eye mask
- objects that make a sound, such as a handbell, alarm, instrument
- science notebook and pencil

Sound helps us explore the world. We can't explore underwater without special equipment, but we can use sounds to explore on land. Try this activity to see if you can lead a partner through a maze!

❯ Set up a simple maze with the chairs or boxes.

❯ Ask your partner to put on a mask.

❯ Try guiding your partner through the maze using one of the sound objects from the list.

❯ **What challenges does your partner encounter?** Was there a sound that worked better? If so, what was it, and why? What didn't work well? Record your observations in your science notebook.

❯ Switch places with your partner and repeat steps 1 through 3.

Try This!

Based on your observations, do you need to move boxes or chairs around? Make different sounds? Try creating a better sound maze and test it.

Audio Patterns

Have you ever listened to someone playing a song on the piano and they hit the wrong note? It just feels wrong, doesn't it? The human brain likes patterns. We like to see patterns and we like to hear them, too. When a sound pattern gets interrupted or goes wrong, we notice it. Why? There are a limited number of sound patterns that go well together. Not all musical notes sound right when played at the same time or close to each other! Our brains know the patterns already because we've been listening all our lives. When one note is off, we can hear it. This gets trickier when we listen to music outside our experience. For example, if you've only ever listened to Eastern music, songs from Western cultures might sound strange the first few times you listen.

FINDING THE OCEAN FLOOR

> **TOOL KIT**
> - plastic tub
> - sand
> - assorted objects including, a cup, lid, and pebbles
> - jug of water
> - string
> - small rock
> - ruler
> - science notebook and pencil

Long ago, sailors didn't have sonar to study underneath the waves. They used a small weight or plumb bob attached to a rope to map the ocean floor. Let's see how it worked.

▶ **Build an ocean floor at the bottom of the tub with the objects and the sand.** Create some underwater mountains and trenches.

▶ **Slowly pour the jug of water into one corner.** If your underwater objects float, weigh them down with the pebbles.

▶ **Tie a 24-inch length of string to the rock.** This is your plumb line.

▶ **Lower the line into one area of the container until it hits the bottom.** Press your fingers around the area of string above the water and pull the string straight up. Measure this wet section with the ruler. Record your observations.

▶ **Repeat step 4 in more areas of your ocean.** In your science notebook, draw a map of what your ocean floor looks like using the measurements. What do the results tell you?

Try This!

Imagine yourself on a research ship in the 1800s. You are in charge of the plumb line. What could get in the way with the accuracy of your work? Write your answers down in your science notebook.

MAKE AN AMPLIFIER

TOOL KIT
- pen or marker
- cardboard toilet paper tube
- scissors
- 2 plastic cups
- glue
- cell phone

Sometimes, we need to turn up the volume. How can we do this without an expensive speaker? Design your own!

> **With your pen, trace the bottom edge of a cell phone onto the middle of the cardboard toilet paper tube.** Be sure to trace all the way around the bottom of the phone so you have a little rectangle shape.

> **Use scissors to cut out the rectangle you have just traced.** Be careful not to cut all the way though both sides of the tube.

> **Trace the end of your toilet paper tube onto one side of a plastic cup and cut out the hole.** This will give you a circle shape. Do the same thing in about the same spot of the other plastic cup. Again, be careful not to cut through both sides of your plastic cup.

> **Place one end of the cardboard tube into the hole in one of the plastic cups.** Put the other end of the cardboard tube into the hole in the other cup.

> **Squeeze a layer of glue all the way around the edges where the cups and the tube meet.** This will keep the tube in place and prevent any sound from escaping through the circles you cut in the cups.

> **Once the glue is dry, insert the phone into the slot you made in the cardboard tube.** Be sure to leave a little open space in the tube so that you don't block any of the holes/speakers on your phone. What happens when you play music on the phone?

Try This!

Will bigger cups make the sound louder? Try it and see!

TRY A CROSSWORD PUZZLE
WHAT'S THAT SOUND?

> **ACROSS**

1. having total or partial hearing loss.

7. an electronic device that increases the strength or power of sounds.

8. faster than the speed of sound.

12. a long period of little or no rain.

14. when an object gently shakes up and down or back and forth.

16. a system that detects objects by bouncing radio waves off them and measuring how long it takes for the waves to return.

18. the ability to find an object by sending out sound waves and listening for them to bounce back.

> **DOWN**

2. the strength of sound waves.

3. a method of using sound pulses to detect objects and to measure the depth of water.

4. the distance from crest to crest in a series of waves.

5. the outer ear in humans and other mammals.

6. vibrations that travel through the air.

9. describes a material that carries electricity easily.

10. how high or low a sound is, depending on its frequency.

11. also known as the voice box, an organ that sits in the neck.

13. a microphone that detects sound waves in the ocean.

15. a branch of science that studies sound and sound waves.

17. the part of the ear where sound waves are turned into electrical signals and sent to the brain for hearing.

GLOSSARY

absorb: to soak up a liquid or take in energy, heat, light, or sound.

acousticophobia: a fear of noise.

acoustics: a branch of science that studies sound and sound waves.

active sonar: a wave of energy sent out to measure how it's reflected back.

amplifier: an electronic device that increases the strength or power of sounds.

amplitude: the strength of sound waves.

archaeologist: a scientist who studies people through the objects they left behind.

architectural acoustics: the science of designing a space to enhance sound within that space.

astronomer: a person who studies objects in the sky such as the sun, moon, planets, and stars.

atmosphere: the mixture of gases surrounding Earth.

atom: the tiniest building block of matter.

attract: when an invisible force pulls things together.

audiologist: a healthcare professional who treats hearing disorders. Audio relates to sound.

auditory: relating to hearing.

beacon: a device that sends out a signal indicating location.

binaural hearing: hearing with two ears.

binocular vision: to use two eyes to see.

biology: the science of life and living things.

brain stem: the lower part of the brain that connects to the spinal cord.

breed: to produce offspring.

chemical reaction: a process where one or more substances are chemically changed and transformed into different substances.

cell: the basic part of a living thing. Cells are so small they can be seen only with a microscope. There are billions of cells in most living things.

climate change: a change in long-term weather patterns, which can happen through natural or manmade processes.

cochlea: the part of the ear where sound waves are turned into electrical signals and sent to the brain for hearing.

cochlear implant: an electronic device to help people with hearing loss to recognize some sounds.

compression wave: waves that are pushed together by the medium through which they travel.

conductive: describes a material that carries electricity easily.

coral reef: an underwater ecosystem that grows in warm ocean waters and is home to millions of creatures.

deaf: having total or partial hearing loss.

decibel (dB): a unit used to measure the loudness of a sound.

dissipate: to scatter in different directions and become less and less.

dissonant: musical notes that do not sound good played together.

dopamine: a chemical in the brain that improves your mood and lowers stress.

Doppler effect: a change in the frequency of waves as an object changes position in relation to an observer.

drought: a long period of little or no rain.

duet: when two people sing together.

GLOSSARY

ear canal: a passage that connects the outer ear to the eardrum.

eardrum: a thin membrane in the middle ear that vibrates in response to sound waves.

ear trumpet: a funnel-shaped device that collects sound waves and leads them into the ear.

echo: a sound caused by the reflection of sound waves from a surface back to the speaker.

echolocation: the ability to find an object by sending out sound waves and listening for them to bounce back.

ecosystem: a community of living and nonliving things and their environment. Living things are plants, animals, and insects. Nonliving things are soil, rocks, and water.

electrode: a conductor through which electricity enters and leaves an object such as a battery.

electrolysis: the process used to capture hydrogen from water using electricity.

electromagnetic: magnetism developed with a current of electricity. Magnetism is a force caused by the motion of electrons that either attracts or repels objects.

energy: the power to work and move.

engineer: someone who uses science, math, and creativity to design and build things.

evolve: to change or develop slowly, during long periods of time.

evolution: the process of living things gradually changing to adapt to the world around them.

expansion: the space between waves as they move apart.

flat note: a note that is half a step lower than the natural note.

forage: to search for food.

force: a push or pull that changes an object's motion.

fossil fuels: a source of energy that comes from plants and animals that lived millions of years ago. These include coal, oil, and natural gas.

frequency: the number of sound waves that pass a fixed point in a second.

gas: a state of matter in which atoms and molecules are spread far apart.

genetic: traits that are passed from parent to child in DNA.

GPS: Global Positioning System, a device that determines its location on Earth using signals sent from different satellites in space.

greenhouse gas: a gas in the atmosphere that traps the sun's heat.

habitat: a plant's or animal's home, which supplies it with food, water, and shelter.

harmony: a pleasing blend of sounds.

hazard: a danger or risk.

hearing aid: a small device that fits in or on the ear, worn by a partially deaf person to amplify sound.

Hertz (Hz): a unit of frequency, equal to one cycle per second.

hormone: a chemical that carries signals from one part of the body to another.

hydrophone: a microphone that detects sound waves in the ocean.

immersive audio: a three-dimensional sound experience that feels like listening to real life.

impaired: weakened or damaged.

GLOSSARY

indigenous: describes people who are native to a place.

Industrial Revolution: a period of time beginning in the late 1700s when people started using machines to make things in large factories.

innovation: a new invention or way of doing something.

insect: an animal that has three body parts and six legs and its skeleton on the outside of its body. Many insects have wings. Grasshoppers, ants, ladybugs, and honeybees are insects.

International Space Station (ISS): a massive space station orbiting Earth where astronauts live, conduct experiments, and study space.

Inuit: a group of indigenous peoples who live in northern Canada, parts of Greenland, and Alaska.

larynx: also known as the voice box, an organ that sits in the neck.

liquid: a state of matter that takes the form of its container and has a fixed volume.

livestock: animals raised for food and other uses.

longitudinal wave: a wave that vibrates parallel to the direction the wave is traveling.

magnetic resonance imaging (MRI): a form of medical imaging that uses high-frequency radio waves and a strong magnetic field.

marine: having to do with the ocean.

matter: any substance that has mass and takes up space, such as air, water, and wood.

medium: a substance, such as air or water, through which energy moves.

microphone: a device that converts sound waves to electrical energy.

microscope: a tool that helps scientists look at objects invisible to the bare eye.

molecule: the smallest amount of something.

navigate: to find the way from one place to another.

neuron: a single nerve cell that carries messages between the brain and other parts of the body.

noise pollution: unwanted or harmful sounds on the land, in the air, or in water.

nuclear reaction: when atoms fuse together or split apart. This releases a large amount of energy.

orchestra: a group of musicians that play a variety of instruments.

organism: a living thing, such as a plant or animal.

oscilloscope: a device that shows the movement of sound waves.

ossicles: three small bones in the middle ear that vibrate in response to sound waves.

passive sonar: a system that detects waves from a source.

patent: a right given to only one inventor to manufacture, use, or sell an invention for a certain number of years.

phenomenon: something seen or observed. Plural is phenomena.

phonograph: a machine that picks up and reproduces the sounds recorded in the grooves cut into a record.

photosynthesis: the process plants use to convert the sun's energy into food.

physicist: a scientist who studies physical forces, including matter, energy, and motion, and how these forces interact with each other.

GLOSSARY

physics: the science of matter, energy, and forces in the universe and how they interact with each other. A scientist who studies physics is a physicist.

pinger: a device that produces a pulsing sound wave.

pinna: the outer ear in humans and other mammals.

pitch: how high or low a sound is, depending on its frequency.

plasma: a state of matter similar to a gas but with temperatures and pressures so high that electrons are stripped away from their atoms and move freely. It is the most common form of matter in the universe.

plumb bob: a small weight attached to a line and used as a level or to measure depth.

plumb line: a length of rope used to find the depth in a body of water.

pollinator: an insect or other animal that transfers pollen from the male part of a flower to the female part of a flower.

predator: an animal that hunts and eats other animals.

pressure waves: waves that create variations of pressure in whatever material they are passing through.

prey: an animal hunted and eaten by other animals.

radar: a system that detects objects by bouncing radio waves off them and measuring how long it takes for the waves to return.

radiation: electromagnetic energy transmitted in the form of rays, waves, or particles from a source, such as the sun.

radio wave: a type of invisible wave used to transmit radio and television signals.

reflect: to bounce off a surface. To redirect something that hits a surface, such as heat, light, or sound.

repel: a force that pushes things away.

rhythm: a regular beat in music.

satellite: a manmade object placed into orbit around Earth, often carrying instruments to gather data.

senses: sight, smell, taste, touch, and hearing are the five senses, all of which give a living thing the ability to learn about its surroundings.

sharp note: a note that is half a step higher than the natural note.

shock wave: a sharp change of pressure moving through the air caused by something moving faster than the speed of sound.

solar energy: energy from the sun.

solar panel: a device used to capture sunlight and convert it to electrical energy.

solid: a state of matter with a definite shape.

sonar: a method of using sound pulses to detect objects and to measure the depth of water.

sonic boom: the sound created by an object traveling through the air faster than the speed of sound.

soothe: to make someone feel calm.

sound: vibrations that travel through matter, which is any substance that has mass and takes up space, such as air, water, and wood.

sound wave: an invisible vibration in the air that you hear as sound.

spatial audio: a method of producing sound so it feels as though it's coming from more than one source.

GLOSSARY

speaker: a device designed to change electrical signals into sound waves that can be heard.

species: a group of organisms that share common traits and can reproduce offspring.

speed of sound: the speed at which sound travels. In the air at sea level, this is 755 miles per hour.

stapes: found in the middle ear, the smallest bone in the human body.

state of matter: the form that matter takes. The four states of matter are solid, liquid, gas, and plasma.

stereophonic hearing: a way of reproducing sound using more than one microphone so the experience is similar to hearing it live.

stethoscope: a tool used by doctors to listen to sounds inside the body.

supersonic: faster than the speed of sound.

symphony: a piece of music written for an orchestra.

technology: tools, methods, and systems used to solve a problem or do work.

thalamus: a part of the brain that acts as a relay station for sensory information.

tissue: a large number of cells in an organism that are similar in form and function and grouped together, such as muscle tissue.

trachea: the windpipe, the tube through which air enters the lungs.

transducer: a device that changes one form of energy into another.

transistor: a device that controls the flow of electricity.

transmitter: a device that sends out radio or television signals.

transponder: a device for receiving a radio signal and automatically transmitting a different signal.

tympanic membrane: the scientific term for the eardrum.

ultrasound imaging: a technique using sound waves that lets doctors see inside a body.

vacuum: a space without air or matter.

vacuum tube: an electronic device that controls the flow of electrons in a vacuum.

varnish: a liquid applied to a surface that dries to form a hard, transparent coating.

vibrate: when an object shakes up and down or back and forth.

vocal cord: one of two thin bands of muscle stretched across the larynx through which air passes in the process of making sound.

volume: the amount of space an object takes up.

wave: a curving movement in water, air, ground, or other object.

wavelength: the distance from crest to crest in a series of waves.

windpipe: also known as the trachea, a tube that runs from the nose and mouth to the lungs.

X-ray: radiation that allows doctors to see your bones.

RESOURCES

Metric Conversions

Use this chart to find the metric equivalents to the English measurements in this book. If you need to know a half measurement, divide by two. If you need to know twice the measurement, multiply by two. How do you find a quarter measurement? How do you find three times the measurement?

English	Metric
1 inch	2.5 centimeters
1 foot	30.5 centimeters
1 yard	0.9 meter
1 mile	1.6 kilometers
1 pound	0.5 kilogram
1 teaspoon	5 milliliters
1 tablespoon	15 milliliters
1 cup	237 milliliters

SELECTED BIBLIOGRAPHY

time.com/6244162/how-sound-can-improve-happiness

journals.plos.org/plosone/article?id=10.1371/journal.pone.0187161

scienceworld.ca/resource/modelling-sound-wave/www.sciencedirect.com/science/article/pii/S0959378022000358

www.bbc.co.uk/programmes/p06tqsg3

divediscover.whoi.edu/history-of-oceanography/the-challenger-expedition/#:~:text=Modern%20oceanography%20began%20with%20the,the%20geology%20of%20the%20seafloor.

arcticwwf.org/threats/underwater-noise

oceanservice.noaa.gov/facts/fish-sonar.html

thinktv.pbslearningmedia.org/subjects/science/physical-sciencewaves-and-light/sound-waves/?rank_by=recency

theatlantic.com/science/archive/2016/01/a-brief-history-of-noise/422481

https://musicalsoundwaves.wordpress.com/the-history-of-sound-waves

britannica.com/science/acoustics/Measuring-the-speed-of-sound

RESOURCES

ESSENTIAL QUESTIONS

Introduction: Why is sound an important part of most people's lives?

Chapter 1: Why do sounds get fainter as you travel farther from the source?

Chapter 2: How does the shape of a creature's ear affect how it hears?

Chapter 3: How do different creatures make different sounds?

Chapter 4: What makes a sound louder or quieter?

Chapter 5: What else are sound waves used for?

BOOKS

Cook, Trevor. *Experiments with Light and Sound*. PowerKids Press, 2011.

Gardner, Robert. *Experimenting with Sound Science Projects*. Enslow, 2013.

Kenney, Karen Latchana. *Sound and Light Waves Investigations*. Lerner, 2017.

Kessler, Colleen. *A Project Guide to Sound*. Mitchell Lane, 2012.

Oxlade, Chris. *Simple Science Experiments: Light and Sound*. Rosen, 2014.

Sohn, Emily. *Adventures in Sound with Max Axiom Super Scientist: 4D An Augmented Reading Science Experience*. Capstone Press, 2019.

Wacholtz, Anthony. *Mummies and Sound*. Capstone Press, 2019.

Yasuda, Anita. *Explore Light and Optics*. Nomad Press, 2016.

WEBSITES

Basics of Sound, Ducksters: *ducksters.com/science/sound101.php*

Kids Connect Sound Facts & Worksheets: *kidskonnect.com/science/sound*

Good Vibration Children's Museum of Houston: *cmhouston.org/good-vibrations*

Science Kids at Home What is Sound: *sciencekidsathome.com/science_topics/what_is_sound.html*

Science Max, Loudest Sound, TVO Kids: *cmhouston.org/good-vibrations*

Science Projects for Kids, Janice VanCleave: *scienceprojectideasforkids.com/sound-facts*

DK findout! Sound: *www.dkfindout.com/uk/science/sound*

StudyJams! Sound: *studyjams.scholastic.com/studyjams/jams/science/energy-light-sound/sound.htm*

Science of Sound for Kids: *sciencekids.co.nz/sound.html*

Nat Geo Kids, Science of Sound Videos: *youtube.com/playlist?list=PLQlnTldJsOZQRzLgW42JXOV_KjtG7TXck*

RESOURCES

QR CODE GLOSSARY

Page 3: *findyourpark.com/about/news/parktracks*

Page 5: *youtube.com/watch?v=a5BZBazNS5Q*

Page 7: *pbs.org/video/curious-crew-sound-vibrations*

Page 8: *vam.ac.uk/articles/leonardo-da-vincis-notebooks?srsltid=AfmBOoqOoDGmiOTjvZ7RoSJd1xuoh_4X-xm7-64DbhTGSsdMUGxvQlF6*

Page 9: *youtube.com/watch?v=4mbypyJjqhk*

Page 11: *soundcities.com*

Page 17: *youtube.com/watch?v=1kjAkuwYx2M*

Page 19: *youtube.com/watch?v=v2pPRiUUnOg*

Page 24: *youtube.com/watch?v=6Dd_pyM-Oj4*

Page 25: *youtube.com/watch?v=4JLNb8-LOB0*

Page 30: *pastmedicalhistory.co.uk/the-story-of-rene-laennec-and-the-first-stethoscope*

Page 31: *francismacdonald.com/new-hamilton*

Page 34: *youtube.com/watch?v=HMXoHKwWmU8*

Page 39: *youtube.com/watch?v=uQfDazQ9Rkg*

Page 39: *youtube.com/watch?v=Ae8VrS_XfO8*

Page 43: *academo.org/demos/virtual-oscilloscope*

Page 46: *dailymotion.com/video/xzrpef*

Page 47: *youtube.com/watch?v=uH0aihGWB8U*

Page 51: *youtube.com/watch?v=ZBg1vfe8P1g*

Page 52: *virtualmusicalinstruments.com*

Page 55: *pulse.berklee.edu/scales/c-major-scale.html*

Page 58: *youtube.com/watch?v=eEKlRUvk9zc*

Page 59: *scmp.com/video/china/2188300/chinese-man-breaks-world-record-highest-vocal-note-male-ear-piercing-singing*

Page 60: *youtube.com/watch?v=GkPrH-dz9LU*

Page 63: *youtube.com/watch?v=_f088FnQOcs*

Page 66: *youtube.com/watch?v=i_rFAo358bU*

Page 68: *noisyplanet.nidcd.nih.gov/have-you-heard/cdc-niosh-app*

Page 69: *youtube.com/watch?v=OknWBh-e7rU*

RESOURCES

QR CODE GLOSSARY

Page 70: *youtube.com/watch?v=gjLu1V4pOqs*

Page 71: *youtube.com/watch?v=laM0Nv8nkw4*

Page 72: *youtube.com/watch?v=i9qMbTba6qk*

Page 73: *youtube.com/watch?v=dEmVeTsQEqQ*

Page 83: *youtube.com/watch?v=lSKA_aTnF5A*

Page 84: *https://seabed2030.org*

Page 85: *youtube.com/watch?v=-fAAxElFeLU*

Page 89: *youtube.com/watch?v=Bt5rCgHN1Gc*

Page 89: *youtube.com/watch?v=Tm-Bq0Gilwk*

INDEX

A

acoustician, 86
acousticophobia, 17
acoustics, 17, 18, 23, 83
activities
  Animal Ears, 46
  Build a Drum, 59
  Build a Wind Instrument, 56
  Collect Sounds, 9
  Conducting Sound, 29
  Explore Sound with a Homemade Guitar, 43
  Finding the Ocean Floor, 93
  Hearing from a Distance, 47
  Make an Amplifier, 94
  Make a Science Notebook, 8
  Modeling a Sound Wave, 32
  Muffling Sound, 77
  Musical Glass, 57
  Music While You Work, 76
  Seeing Molecules, 12
  Seeing Sound Waves, 31
  Sonar Sound Maze, 92
  Sound Detective, 11
  Sound Maker, 58
  Sound Story, 74
  Stethoscope Science, 30
  String Telephone, 28
  Try a Crossword Puzzle: What's That Sound?, 95
  Tune Booster, 75
  Vibrating Drum, 44
  Warbling Wineglasses, 60–61
  What's That Sound?, 10
  Where's That Sound?, 45
aircraft, v, 66–67, 68, 71
amplitude, 15, 63–64
animals
  echolocation by, 26, 41–42, 80, 85
  hearing of, iv, 27, 36, 39, 41, 42, 46–47
  marine, 78, 84–86, 87
  noise effects on, 69, 86
Aristotle, iv, 16, 82
audio engineers, 77
audio patterns, 92

B

Bell, Alexander Graham, iv, 64
binaural hearing, 90–91
Boethius, iv
Boyle, Robert, iv, 17, 20, 21
brain function, 35, 39, 45, 90, 92

INDEX

C
Challenger, HMS, 81–82
climate change, 87–88
cochlear implants, v, 38–39, 41
Colladon, Daniel, 82
compression waves. *See* sound waves

D
Dance, Helen Oakley, v
da Vinci, Leonardo, iv, 8, 82
decibels, 64
Donald, Ian, v
Doppler, Christian/Doppler effect, iv, 18–19

E
ears
  for hearing, 33–35, 36, 39, 42, 44–46, 76, 90
  hearing aids in, v, 36–39, 41
  protection of, 64–66, 69
ear trumpets, 37
echoes, 23–25, 31
echolocation, 26–27, 41–42, 79–80, 85. *See also* sonar
electromagnetic waves, 21–22, 25
energy, 3–5, 14, 21, 62–64

F
Fletcher, Alice Cunningham, v
Forest 404, 73
Franklin, Ben, 58, 60, 61
frequency, iv, 15, 24, 43, 50

G
Galilei, Galileo, iv, 17
Galton, Francis, iv
Gassendi, Pierre, iv
glass armonica, 58, 60, 61
Golconda fort, 23

H
Hamilton Mausoleum, 24
hearing, 33–47
  animals' ability of, iv, 27, 36, 39, 41, 42, 46–47
  binaural, 90–91
  ears for, 33–35, 36, 39, 42, 44–46, 76, 90
  immersive audio and, v, 88, 89–91
  impairment of, v, 36–39, 41, 44
  plants' ability of, 54
  protection of, 64–66, 69
  visual impairment and, 40–42
hearing aids, v, 36–39, 41
Hertz, Heinrich/Hertz, 24
Hodgson, Leslie, 41
Hooke, Robert, iv, 17, 20, 21
Hughes, Megan Watts, v
Hutchinson, Miller Reese, 37

I
immersive audio, v, 88, 89–91
instruments, musical, 43, 52, 53–61, 63

K
Kelso Dunes, 9
Kish, Daniel, 41–42, 47

L
Laennec, René, 30
larynx, 49–51. *See also* vocal cords
longitudinal waves. *See* sound waves

M
Macdonald, Francis, 31
Mach, Ernst/Mach, v, 71
marine bioacousticians, 86
matter, 5–7, 20–21
Mersenne, Marin, 17
molecules, 5–7, 12, 14–15, 16, 21, 22–23

music
  amount and variety of, 3
  audio engineers in, 77
  audio patterns in, 92
  echoes in, 31
  history of study of, v, 16–17
  immersive audio with, v, 88, 89–91
  instruments for playing, 43, 52, 53–61, 63
  pitch in. *See* pitch
  sound waves creating, 14–15, 16–17
  throat singing as, 51
  vibrations creating, 5, 6, 43, 54
  volume of, 62–64, 76

N
nature, sounds of, 72–73
Newton, Isaac, iv
Nixon, Lewis, v, 82
noise/noise pollution, 67–71, 72, 86, 87
Nollet, Jean-Antoine, 4

O
ocean
  climate change effects on, 87–88
  marine animals in, 78, 84–86, 87
  technology to explore, v, 26–27, 78–84, 85, 88, 93
  waves in, 14
oscilloscopes, 43

P
pitch, 48–61
  hearing of, 44, 59
  of instruments, 52, 53–61
  sound waves and, 15, 19
  unique personal factors affecting, 50–52
  voice box, vocal cords, and, 48, 49–51
plants, 54, 69
Pythagoras, iv, 16

INDEX

R
radiologists, 26
radio waves, 18, 20, 22, 24

S
Sabine, Wallace, 18
Seabed 2030, 84
sonar, v, 26–27, 78–84, 92
sonic booms, 67, 68, 71
soothing sounds, 72–73
sound
  amount and variety of, 1–3
  definition of, 2
  as energy, 3–5, 14, 21, 62–64
  fear of, 17
  hearing of. *See* hearing
  history of study of, iv–v, 16–19
  matter, molecules, and, 5–7, 12, 14–15, 16, 20–21, 22–23
  musical. *See* music
  noise of, 67–71, 72, 86, 87
  pitch of. *See* pitch
  soothing, 72–73
  sound waves and. *See* sound waves
  in space, 21–23
  speed of, iv–v, 66–67, 71, 85
  technology for. *See* sound technology
  volume of, 19, 62–66, 67, 75–77, 94
  word for, 12
sound engineers, 77
sound technology, 78–95
  climate change and, 87–88
  hearing and, 38. *See also* hearing aids
  immersive audio with, v, 88, 89–91
  marine animals and, 78, 84–86, 87
  sonar as, v, 26–27, 78–84, 92

sound waves, 13–32
  amplitude of, 15, 63–64
  anatomy of, 14–15, 70
  definition of, 6
  echoes of, 23–25, 31
  echolocation using, 26–27, 41–42, 79–80, 85. *See also* sonar
  frequency of, iv, 15, 24, 43, 50
  history of study of, iv–v, 16–19
  matter, molecules, and, 6–7, 14–15, 16, 20–21, 22–23
  sonic booms and, 67, 68, 71
  in space, 21–23
  technology using. *See* sound technology
  travel of, 20–21
  vibrations creating, 6, 14, 21, 25, 31. *See also* vibrations
  wavelength of, 15
space, sound in, 21–23
Spallanzani, Lazzaro, iv
speech language pathologists, 40
speed of sound, iv–v, 66–67, 71, 85
stethoscopes, 30

T
taiko drums, 63
technology. *See* sound technology
telephones, iv, 18, 20, 28, 44
throat singing, 51
Tiso, Robert, 60

U
ultrasound imaging, v, 24–25

V
vacuum, 17, 21
vibrations
  definition of, 4
  energy and, 4–5, 63
  hearing and, 35, 38, 43–44, 76
  music created with, 5, 6, 43, 54
  pitch and, 48–50
  sound waves and, 6, 14, 21, 25, 31. *See also* sound waves
  volume and, 63, 75
vocal cords, 48, 49–51
voice box, 49–51. *See also* vocal cords
volume, 19, 62–66, 67, 75–77, 94

W
Xialong, Wang, 59
water
  molecules of, 5, 12, 22–23
  sound through, v, 4–5, 26–27, 29, 46, 57, 78–88
  waves of, iv, 14
wavelength, 15. *See also* sound waves

Y
Yeager, Chuck, v, 66–67